Heidi has captured "God's got this" in absolutely every page of this book. As I am reading through her book, I am challenged to remember that whenever and in whatever circumstances we face, whether it is healing in body, soul, or spirit, or perhaps a financial or family crisis, our heavenly Father has us in the palm of His hand, and no circumstance is too hard for Him. These are stories of real people encountering a very big God, and my prayer for you as you read through it is that you will grow in faith and trust that "God's got this" for you too.

CAROL ARNOTT, Catch the Fire

I have a friend who's a businessman, and he spent a couple of weeks in Mozambique with Rolland and Heidi Baker. After returning to his beautiful home and significant business venture, he found himself weeping at the most awkward times. Concerned, he wondered what was happening. He realized he missed Jesus. Literally. It wasn't that Jesus wasn't with him. He was a true, radical believer. But the presence of Jesus upon Heidi Baker's life is so tangible that he hungered for the reality of Jesus more than ever before. Heidi's devotional, *God's Got This*, will have a similar impact on all who read it. It is filled with stories of surrendered trust, frighteningly bold risks, and the supernatural interventions of a loving God. These testimonies from her own life and the lives of those around her reveal God's goodness in such an astounding way that worship from surrender is our only reasonable response.

BILL JOHNSON, Bethel Church, Redding, CA
Author of *Born for Significance* and *The Way of Life*

I am so happy Dr. Heidi Baker has put together this book of testimonies about partnering with God to overcome life's toughest challenges. Heidi is a person who lives in the miraculous presence of Jesus. She has seen firsthand how Jesus heals the blind, raises the dead, and brings multitudes into His kingdom of grace and light. She has also comforted those who have lost absolutely everything. As you read these stories of great trials and great victories from around the world, you will be encouraged to cling to God no matter what. Whatever you are going through, let these words minister to your heart and prophesy hope into your situation.

STACEY CAMPBELL, Shiloh Global

Heidi Baker loves reading devotionals, and now she has written a great devotional that brings peace to troubled hearts, hope for those facing the clouds of uncertainty, and faith for those being asked to step out of their boats of security and walk on the water to Jesus. I love Heidi and her passionate devotion to Jesus. Her new devotional, *God's Got This*, is a great book. I highly recommend it to all. Her faith walks in the midst of persecution and poverty as she and her husband, Rolland, have lived and served on four continents. Out of the richness of their experiences with God, which are mind-blowingly amazing, and her life of devotion she has written her devotional book. This would be a great introduction to Heidi that you could give to a friend who may not know about her amazing life.

RANDY CLARK, Global Awakening

Heidi Baker is a great friend and one of my absolute heroes of the faith. She's a hero not only because of what she has done for God but also because she has always trusted God in the midst of absolutely impossible circumstances. This devotional is all those years and lessons packed into a book. As I read through this devotional, it just oozes courage, courage, courage as the stories and revelations here highlight how God never fails us and always provides more than what we need, no matter what we face. It's filled with wild acts of faith, hardship where the "God of all comfort" comes close to us, and testimonies where there was no answer left, then God did great miracles. As you read this book, I'm certain you'll be filled with more assurance of His nature, more deep trust in what He can do, and a lifting of courage in your personal calling to change history for Jesus. With our God, *all* things are possible.

BEN FITZGERALD, Senior Leader, Awakening Europe

I honestly cannot say enough good things about Heidi's new devotional. *God's Got This* offers tender stories of real-life people and the struggles they encounter yet victories that offer a renewed sense of hope to all. *God's Got This* is truly a refreshing read as it offers not only sound teaching but also a practical application for all readers in every walk of life. It stirs up hope amid uncertainty. It attests to God's faithfulness through every storm.

WILL HART, Iris Global CEO

Heidi's life reflects an unwavering trust in God as the One who miraculously provides. In her life choice to walk the canyon floor in loyal relationships with the community of Mozambique, she has empowered a generation of believers into radical love for Him and others. *God's Got This* encourages a new level of trust in Him amid a convulsing world.

HEATHER JOHNSTON, Founder and Executive Director
JH Israel and US Israel Education Association

God's Got This

40 Devotions of Courageous Faith

Heidi Baker

BroadStreet

PUBLISHING

BroadStreet Publishing® Group, LLC
Savage, Minnesota, USA
BroadStreetPublishing.com

God's Got This: 40 Devotions of Courageous Faith
Copyright © 2021 Heidi Baker

978-1-4245-6195-7 (faux leather)
978-1-4245-6196-4 (e-book)

Stock or custom editions of BroadStreet Publishing titles may be purchased in bulk for educational, business, ministry, fundraising, or sales promotional use. For information, please email orders@broadstreetpublishing.com.

Design and typesetting | garborgdesign.com

Printed in China
21 22 23 24 25 5 4 3 2 1

I would like to dedicate this book with great love and gratitude to Rolland, Elisha, Crystalyn, and Brock, who have traveled this journey through the years with me, always believing that God's got this! I also want to dedicate this book to our big, cherished Mozambican family who adopted us as their very own: thank you. Finally, I dedicate this book to my adventurous, super fun granddaughter, Zoe Joy Leora, and our grandson, Lev Leon. May you always know that no matter what the storms of life may be, God is good and loving and faithful, and God's got this. I love you all so much, and you bring my heart joy.

Our beautiful, blended family

CONTENTS

FOREWORD

Truth is so much better than fiction. We all like hearing about true-life stories of heroism and love. They move us, challenge us, and convict us. The stories and truths you are about to read in this devotional are all real-life stories of the triumph of love. The book you hold in your hand is a testimony of God's faithfulness and His endless love for the souls of women and men. It is full of insight that will change your life and enlarge your heart for God.

Missionaries are a unique breed. They leave behind what most of us chase after. God calls missionaries to leave family and lands behind to further the cause of the kingdom of God. They step out in faith to witness the miraculous. They live in different nations, face different tests and trials, and adapt to different cultures. Missionaries experience pressures that most of us will never have to encounter. They lay down their lives for the sake of the gospel. I love missionaries, don't you? Heidi and Rolland Baker are examples of God-drenched lovers of God, missionaries who have given their lives to touch the poor and needy of the earth, wherever they may be found.

Today, the nations of the earth are crying out for God's intervention. Famines, wars, pandemics, and political upheavals can be seen on a global scale. Like never before in human history, we need to know that God's got this! We need the confidence that God not only sees our need but also that His heart is moved to bless and heal. Does God really care about you and me? Does He really care about the nations of the earth? Of course, He does! The cross is the answer to the questions of our hearts. Millions and millions of believers today can testify to God's mercy that is renewed every morning.

John's Gospel unveils to us the heart of Jesus. We see Him in chapter 11 standing at the sealed tomb of His dear friend Lazarus. As He looks around and sees the broken hearts of Lazarus' sisters, Mary and Martha, Jesus begins to sob. His heart melted with compassion for them in their grief. John was there to see it and wrote, "Tears streamed down Jesus' face" (John 11:35).

This scene can be superimposed over the need of the world today. Jesus is still moved deeply and filled with compassion for the people of the world. Yes, God's got this! What troubles you troubles Him. He took your pain and trouble so that you can live a life gloriously free and without worry. The whole world is in His hands, and so are you!

What we need is the gospel of the kingdom of God to blanket the earth. It is a gospel of God's endless grace, eternal love, and exciting power. Miracles are part and parcel of the good news we preach today. There is nothing impossible with God, no one out of God's reach, and no nation that cannot be revived and transformed by His power-driven hands. The lives of Heidi and Rolland Baker are testimonies of this power. They have witnessed great miracles and glory invasions. They have seen mass conversions and miracle breakthroughs. The world today is greatly blessed by the lives of these two world changers. Their testimony can be your testimony.

The God of glory lives in you and wants you to be an outlet of his power and love. Let your heart soar as you read this book. More than a devotional, it is a road map for you to turn to and find the heart of God—our wonderful God who can do more than we ask or dream. Take the next forty days and go deep. May the message contained in these pages challenge and change us!

DR. BRIAN SIMMONS
The Passion Translation Project

INTRODUCTION

I've been deeply inspired by the anointed and powerful lives of men and women who fix their eyes on Jesus through the trials of life and never give up, knowing God's got this. We interviewed courageous believers and asked them, "What did you overcome with God's help?" The following forty stories are authentic responses. We vulnerably share our deepest fears and the hardest parts of some of the most challenging times of our lives. I've been profoundly impacted by The Passion Translation, so we've chosen to mostly use this fresh, heart-level translation of the Bible.

The resilience, trust, tenacity, intimacy, and joy that my friends have expressed through their extraordinary stories are powerful testimonies that are not only moving but also reassuring that God's utterly totally, and always got this. My prayer, from Philippians, is that you would "Tell [God] every detail of your life, then God's wonderful peace that transcends human understanding, will make the answers known to you through Jesus Christ. So keep your thoughts continually fixed on all that is authentic and real, honorable and admirable, beautiful and respectful, pure and holy, merciful and kind. And fasten your thoughts on every glorious work of God, praising him always" (Philippians 4:6–8).

Share and Care

If you keep my commands, you will live in my love,
just as I have kept my Father's commands,
for I continually live nourished and
empowered by his love.

JOHN 15:10

My first days in Mozambique were extremely difficult. The nation was war-torn, the streets lined with burned cars and destroyed buildings. A Bible school allowed me to stay in their building but only for three nights. Rolland, Elisha, and Crystalyn hadn't arrived yet, and there were no cell phones to call anyone. I had nowhere to stay, and I was quickly running out of money and food. I sat outside in the dirt near a water spigot, crying out to Jesus for help and leaning on God alone.

Something inside of me knew that God had called us to this nation. I knew He wanted me to learn the language of the people and the language of the Holy Spirit, and I knew that He would lead us. Near that spigot, I sensed He wanted me to trust Him more. I remembered how He always provided for us before. Suddenly a woman with her hair in a bun, wearing a long, flowered skirt and tennis shoes ran up and tossed me a set of keys. She asked me to take care of her flat while she traveled up north. She told me to eat the food so that the rats wouldn't get it. I assumed she was a missionary, but she left without even telling me her name or where her flat was. It was wild. I had the keys but no address.

I asked for help from a man standing nearby. We could barely communicate, but when he said his name was Lazarus, I knew we'd be okay. He knew the woman and helped me find her flat. There were no road signs, but we somehow made it to her place just after the gas dial hit zero. As I opened the door, I burst into tears. I had barely slept in three days because car thieves continually triggered my truck's alarm. I was too exhausted to eat. I just slept. After that, Lazarus and his wife became my dear friends. Along with the street children, they helped teach me their languages. They showed me the beauty and patience of the Mozambican people.

During this process, my trust in God reached a new level. The Lord is in control. He will take care of us. If He asks you to do something, He is going to provide for you. He is going to make a way for you, but He wants you to learn the language of the Holy Spirit. God Himself will help you fulfill your assignment. He also calls you to

minister with those in the body of Christ that He is calling to work alongside of you.

Right now, believers all over the world can learn from
the believers in the book of Acts. We need to continue
sharing like they did: in a radical way. This sharing is also
a beautiful part of Mozambican culture; even people who
are extremely poor share what they have. I believe we
are living in an unprecedented time of ever more merciful sharing and compassionate caring across the body of
Christ worldwide.

*Jesus, show me what love looks like here on
earth. Holy Spirit, empower me to be merciful,
generous, and compassionate. I trust in your
eternal faithfulness. Draw me into your heart
and open my eyes to see those who are in need.*

- Share: "All the believers were one in mind and heart. Selfishness was not a part of their community, for they shared everything they had with one another" (Acts 4:32).

- Learn the language of the Holy Spirit: "We must live in the Holy Spirit and follow after him" (Galatians 5:25).

- Rest. The Lord is the author and the finisher. He starts things and finishes them too. He knows the ending of the story. See Hebrews 12:1–3.

Baptisms on the Iris Zimpeto base in Maputo

Always Enough

As Jesus sat down, he looked out and saw the massive crowd of people scrambling up the hill, for they wanted to be near him. So he turned to Philip and said, "Where will we buy enough food to feed all these people?"

JOHN 6:5

In John 6, we read the story of Jesus feeding five thousand people by multiplying five loaves of bread and two fish that a small boy had given him. This story moves me deeply because we regularly minister to crowds of thousands of hungry people in Mozambique. You see, a war in the northern part of the country has forced hundreds of thousands of people to flee for their lives with whatever they are able to carry. Multitudes of these internally displaced people have fled to Cabo Delgado, where we live. They arrive traumatized, desperate, and hungry. Our teams help by leading spiritual and physical food distribution each week, and we often rely on God's miraculous provision.

We once prepared a distribution of food aid for five hundred families staying on our Glory Garden base. It was the rainy season in Mozambique, and as we pulled up to the base, we saw thousands upon thousands of families standing outside in the torrential downpour, waiting for us to distribute food. Anxious and famished, the people started to push down the door to our warehouse. We feared a riot might break out, leaving people badly injured. And it pained my heart to see so many beautiful women, who were created in the image of God, crawling on their hands and knees in monsoon rains, frantically scraping a few beans and grains of wet rice into their T-shirts.

Overwhelmed, my team and I looked at one another, wondering what to do. How would we feed thousands of families when we only had enough food for five hundred? I sensed the Lord telling me to stop and pray with my Mozambican team. We laid hands on the food and cried out to God. We needed His strategy and peace. As we prayed, I remembered that we had many boxes of MannaPacks, which are bags of nutrient-dense food, stored at our Maringanha base. I called our Maringanha team and asked them to deliver the boxes, but they feared it would be impossible to reach us through the heavy rains and thick mud. I urged them to trust God and try. Remarkably, the truck trudged through the mud and rain and parked under our church roof to keep the food dry as we placed it into the hands of hungry, destitute men, women, and children.

Whenever you find yourself in a situation that seems bigger than you, pause for a moment in the secret place and listen for God's plan. He has the solution, and we are called to stop long enough to listen to it. I was full of faith that God had a strategy for us on that rainy, miraculous day. We felt entirely overwhelmed, but then the Lord powerfully showed us exactly what to do.

As the cofounder of Iris Global, I feel passionately compelled to believe that God will pass food through our hands and into the hands of the hungry, the sick, the dying, the broken, and the displaced. Now we feed approximately thirty thousand people per day in Cabo Delgado, and we feel God encouraging us to believe for more. What is God encouraging you to believe?

God, thank You that You already have a solution for every challenge I will face. Help me to pause in the secret place and listen. Download Your plans to me today and share your creative solutions with me. I trust in You—completely.

- Fix your eyes on Jesus and pause: "Surrender your anxiety. Be still and realize that I am God" (Psalm 46:10).

- Listen for God's plan: "Jesus already knew what he was about to do, but he said this to stretch Philip's faith" (John 6:6).

- Trust God's creative solution: "Who are they that live in the holy fear of Yahweh? You will show them the right path to take" (Psalm 25:12).

Our distribution of food aid on our Glory Garden base

DAY 3

The Truth Is Jesus

When the disciples were together, with the doors locked
for fear of the Jewish leaders, Jesus came and stood among
them and said, "Peace be with you!" After he said this,
he showed them his hands and side.

JOHN 20:19–20 NIV

Brother Yun is a dear friend who has ministered deeply to our movement in Mozambique, and even though he has suffered far more torture than most humans, he is one of the most joyful people I've ever met. He also understands what so many believers are experiencing in Northern Mozambique. During his third stint in Chinese prison for spreading the gospel, he and his friend, Peter, lived in fear much like the disciples in John 20. Brother Yun's legs had been broken, and he and Peter worried the police would eventually execute them. They did not doubt Jesus, but they were scared nonetheless.

God spoke to Peter and told him to tell Brother Yun to leave prison. Peter was reluctant to share this with Brother Yun, as trying to escape high security prison would surely end in death. But Peter obeyed and told Brother Yun what God had said. *Impossible*, Brother Yun had thought. How would he get past the locks? And even if he did, his legs were broken, and the guards might kill him. But Brother Yun felt God say, *The prison is a fact. Everything you thought is a fact. But I am the truth.*

Brother Yun thought of his wife and remembered his calling to preach the gospel. He also understood that if he were to die, then he would die for Christ. He overcame his fear, stood up, and walked right out of prison. God miraculously opened the doors. In John 20:19 the doors behind the disciples were also locked. This was a fact. The truth is that Jesus walked through the doors and said, "Peace be with you." Jesus Christ is the truth, and with this truth there is freedom.

During personal trials, our thoughts are our biggest enemy. If your mind or heart doubts, open your mouth and declare what God says. Say aloud, "God's got this. God can do this. God will do this." It's not about whether God can do it or not; He can! The important thing is whether you believe He intends to do everything He says in your life.

By God's grace, Brother Yun saw that what God declares will come to pass. Sometimes it takes years; sometimes it takes days, but His Word will bear fruit.

Brother Yun's advice for overcoming fear, persecution, and difficulty is to look to Jesus. Look at the wounds on His hands and on His side. He suffered and died for us. Whatever you are going through, look up. If you look up at Jesus, then He will fill you with eternal joy. He will speak to you about your calling and give you everything you need. He will also give you an eternal perspective. We live, or die, for Christ. He is the only truth.

Jesus, I look up to You. I see Your hands and Your side. You suffered and died for me. I receive power and confidence to overcome my thoughts and my fears. Help me to stand up and overcome.

- Feed your faith: "We are certainly not those who are held back by fear and perish; we are among those who have faith and experience true life!" (Hebrews 10:39).

- Obey: "You show that you are my intimate friends when you obey all that I command you" (John 15:14).

- "Be cheerful with joyous celebration in every season of life. Let joy overflow, for you are united with the Anointed One!" (Philippians 4:4).

Brother Yun and Heidi on outreach in Northern Mozambique

Stand Firm, Storm Riders

*Don't be pulled in different directions or worried about
a thing. Be saturated in prayer throughout each day,
offering your faith-filled requests before God with
overflowing gratitude.*

PHILIPPIANS 4:6

Nathan and Sarah Kotzur have been part of our Iris family for many years. They led our Harvest school in Mozambique and later moved to Los Angeles with a vision to reach the people of Hollywood with God's love. While in LA, they founded and continue to lead our Iris LA Film, Acting, and Music (ILA FAM) schools. Their first son, Israel, my godson, was also born there.

Before Israel was born and before they had moved to Los Angeles, God gave Sarah an impression of her future son as a five-year-old boy. We had prayed together for two years for her to conceive, and by the grace of God, our prayers were fulfilled. However, when Israel was six months old, his parents had to rush him to the emergency room on eight different occasions for life-threatening conditions. The hardest part for Nathan was watching his wife suffer over and over. The hardest part for Sarah was watching her promised son, whom she had waited and longed for, experience tremendous pain and distress. Naturally, they were terrified of losing him.

Nathan and Sarah felt stripped of all control—except to trust in the unfailing love of Christ. Then Sarah had a vision where everything important in their lives was floating in space, but Jesus stood firmly on a rock in the center. He was the only immovable thing. He said, *Sarah you can either spend your life in fear because everything here is shakable, or you can spend your life in confidence that I AM completely unshakable. I AM your only constant.*

They knew that God had to come first, even above promises of great destiny or Israel's healing, so they chose to stand firm in His goodness and love, no matter what. They would charge through whatever storms came their way with God as their anchor. Battle after battle, Sarah held on to the impression of five-year-old Israel. Nathan and Sarah fixed their eyes on Jesus and declared His promises. They chose to be storm riders.

From Mozambique, we prayed, *Life, life, life!* I remember pacing up and down while praying. It felt like we prayed for an eternity, but God gave us a strong impression that Israel would live. Sure enough, Jesus sustained

Israel's life. Time and again, Israel was supernaturally delivered, including the time he suffered third-degree burns. His skin miraculously grew back in three days, and the doctors canceled his scheduled surgeries.

In every storm, you have a choice. You can panic and give in to fear, or you can push forward in faith. We are not fair-weather sailors; we are the ones who are willing to weather storms, and Jesus knows how to anchor us when the waves of life crash all around us. If it feels like the floor has fallen out from under your very feet, choose trust. Bring every concern straight to God with thanksgiving. That is where we find relief. Even when we do not understand why certain things are happening, we stay in the Word and trust that His grace is sufficient. God is not cruel. Consider the story of Job, who experienced all kinds of terror before God granted him blessings and fruitfulness. No matter how big the storm, remember that He is with you, and you are loved. He is unshakable!

Jesus, You are our only constant. We want to see You face-to-face because when we truly understand Your beauty, we won't be afraid. We are storm riders, the ones who make it through full of faith!

- Worship God, your Rock: "They remembered that God, the Mighty One, was their strong protector, the Hero-God who would come to their rescue" (Psalm 78:35).

- Lean on your friends and family. We can't get through storms all alone. (See Ecclesiastes 4:9–12)

- Laugh: "A joyful, cheerful heart brings healing to both body and soul" (Proverbs 17:22).

Heidi and the Kotzur family
(Israel is pictured in front of Heidi)

God Is Sovereign

"For I know the plans I have for you," declares the LORD,
"plans to prosper you and not to harm you,
plans to give you hope and a future."
JEREMIAH 29:11 NIV

In 2001, a serious cholera outbreak erupted near our base in Maputo. Cholera is a highly infectious, deadly disease that causes rapid loss of bodily fluids. Seventy of our pastors and children became infected from contaminated lettuce. Military police armed with machine guns came to our base, blaming us for the outbreak. We told them we believed God would heal everyone.

Pastor Surpresa Sithole, our dear friend and a leader at Iris, went with me to the cholera isolation tent to pray. We brought Coca-Cola, Maria biscuit cookies, and mineral water. We did not wear gloves, masks, or gowns. Patients defecated and vomited on us, but cheek to cheek we embraced them in prayer. Neither of us felt afraid.

Our only concern was that the military police might kick us out before we could complete our mission.

Doctors mocked us. They didn't believe in the healing power of God. Doctor Joanna, a Mozambican atheist, said we were stupid and would surely die. Day one, we saw the first breakthrough. Several people were healed and left the cholera tent. Day two, more of our pastors and children left the tent completely healed. Within three days, God miraculously cleared the tents. We shared Coca-Cola and cookies with the patients whom we didn't know. Each one felt the love and kindness of God. After every single person left the cholera tent completely healed, Dr. Joanna told me, "Your God is God," and she came to faith in Jesus. For the next two years, she worked with us in our medical clinic.

In that tent, God assured Pastor Surpresa that He was with us powerfully and reminded him of Jeremiah 29:11: His plans give us hope and a future. As believers, we are carriers of the message of hope in every circumstance. Especially in times when people are confused and afraid of dying, we are reminded of Hebrews 10:23: "Now we must cling tightly to the hope that lives within us, knowing that God always keeps his promises!"

We wait on God to receive His peace and courage, and then His love compels us to action. His love sent us to that tent full of seriously ill people, and as we prayed and looked into each pair of sunken eyes, we felt the Father's love and compassion for them. Then we watched people return to health—smiling, laughing, and speaking—and our faith increased exponentially. God is in charge. He is sovereign, and the more we engage with Him, the more we become one with Him and feel His compassion for others. This brings us joy during even the most challenging circumstances. We get face-to-face with God and face-to-face with those who are suffering. Then we carry His radical love, hope, and compassion to those in need.

Jesus, thank You for Your victory on the cross.
Thank You for Your compassion and love that
bring supernatural healing. Compel my heart
to carry Your message of hope to those who
are suffering, as I trust in You.

- Don't make a final decision based on temporary circumstances. Fight for your joy. Fight for your faith.

- Dig Deep: "Even when their paths wind through the dark valley of tears, they dig deep to find a pleasant pool where others find only pain" (Psalm 84:6).

- "Discover creative ways to encourage others and to motivate them toward acts of compassion, doing beautiful works as expressions of love" (Hebrews 10:24).

Pastor Surpresa and his wife, Tryphina

Take the First Step

As you go into all the world, preach openly the wonderful
news of the gospel to the entire human race!
MARK 16:15

After ministering in southern Mozambique for eight years, we felt called to a new destination. It all started in Red Deer, Canada, at a conference in God's strong presence. I felt the Lord saying, *Go and get my lost Makua bride.* I asked my husband to research the Makua. We were excited to learn they were the most unreached people group in northern Mozambique. I quickly realized this meant leaving the south and starting over again. The weight of my yes to God hit me. I had been working in the city garbage dump for eight years, sharing the gospel and building deep friendships. We had a wonderful team to put in charge, but it was still painful to say goodbye. My heart broke over leaving the children we rescued from the streets, so we brought fifty of them with us.

We took the first step to visit Pemba, where we discovered a great number of Makua people living on the stunning coastline, although it was the poorest province in the poorest nation. I found it challenging to believe God would call us somewhere so beautiful because I had always felt my calling was to squalor ministry. We shared the gospel with beach vendors selling necklaces, and they came to faith instantly. Next, we looked at properties. Most of the properties were mud huts, but God miraculously provided a two-bedroom block house for us. We met a man willing to sell a plot of land for Iris for $700 and a suit. I searched sweltering street markets all day and found trousers, a shirt, a tie, and shoes. The man loved them. We had a deal.

The transition stretched us more than anything in our lives. We were stoned on outreaches and received death threats. We experienced extreme heat, power outages, and severe water shortages. We had surrounded ourselves with the poorest people on the planet and often felt overwhelmed trying to meet their needs. Nevertheless, we bonded deeply with our Mozambican team and faced the challenges together.

In Pemba, we started the base and Harvest ministry school for national and international students. We sent one to four outreach teams per week throughout the province for almost fifteen years. We had no idea a war with radical insurgents would break out and that believers would be persecuted, but God knew. He had a plan to raise powerful Mozambican leaders to continue the work of the gospel. Our Harvest school can no longer meet in Mozambique, but mercifully, Rolland and I are still here and ministering with our courageous teams.

When you sense it's time for a transition, it's important to surround yourself with strong believers for their wise counsel and prayer support. Never leave somewhere feeling burned out, angry, or upset. Transition with peace, love, and grace in your heart. When you're ready, take the first step in faith but don't be in a rush. It took us a full year to raise up the leaders in the south and move north. And even when the unexpected happens, I can truly tell you God's got this. He is sovereign, and you can trust Him in the storm.

God, give me courage to take the first step by faith. Even when things look impossible and nothing like I expected, You've still got this. You aren't taken by surprise. You are with me in every transition and every season.

- Take the first step in faith: "Travel light, and don't even pack an extra change of clothes in your backpack. Trust God for everything" (Matthew 10:10).

- Finish well. Complete your season with peace in your heart and transition in God's timing, not in a rush. "Listen well to wise counsel" in transitions (Proverbs 19:20).

- Trust that God has a plan and is truly sovereign: "God's heavenly throne is eternal, secure, and strong, and his sovereignty rules the entire universe" (Psalm 103:19).

A child worshipping in Maputo, Mozambique
"Blessed are the pure in heart, for they will see God."

MATTHEW 5:8 NIV

The Other Side of Sorrow

Truly, truly, I say to you, unless a grain of wheat
falls into the earth and dies, it remains alone;
but if it dies, it bears much fruit.

JOHN 12:24 ESV

Rebekah and Daryl Martin served with Iris Malawi for several years. Daryl was a passionate photographer and very familiar with the local wildlife reserve, and he loved driving visitors on safari. One day, after receiving a new camera, he brought Rebekah to the reserve on a date to photograph elephants and the sunset.

After searching a long time for an elephant herd, they spotted one in the distance. Daryl exited the car and walked quickly toward the majestic beasts. Rebekah started following but suddenly sensed a warning: *Stop. If you go, your children won't have a parent.* She called to Daryl to stop, but he was distracted, searching for the perfect photograph. Praying, she sensed the warning a second time. Again, she called to Daryl, but he was already too far away to hear her.

Suddenly, an elephant trumpeted and charged. Daryl ran, but she lost sight of him in the bush. Panicking, Rebekah tried to drive after him, but the terrain was too rough for the vehicle. Frantic, she drove back to the entrance and begged the reserve staff for help. They grabbed their guns and went after him. She imagined Daryl injured and alone and hoped he understood that she had gone for help.

The staff searched for what felt like an eternity. At last, they returned with their heads hung low. She sensed God asking her, *If you lose Daryl, will you still walk with Me?* She thought, *No, no, no, it couldn't be true.* But the staff said, "We found your husband" and drove her to his body.

The following events were a blur. Friends brought Rebekah home and prayed with her. To God, to herself, and to her family, she declared, "We are not going to go dark in this. We will not accuse God of anything but goodness. We will not anesthetize our pain or allow ourselves to get stuck in our grief. We have a call on our lives. We will get through this with God." It was the hardest night of her life. She woke to Malawian mourning songs, and at sunset Daryl was laid to rest. Rebekah noticed a nearby field that was ready for harvest and remembered John 12:24: God promised a harvest from the tragedy.

She and her children returned to the USA. Friends from around the world surrounded and blessed them. Through tears and sleepless nights, they stayed close to God. A year later, they visited Malawi and could truly rejoice again. Iris children said Daryl gave them the gift of grieving for the first time, for him and for their own tragedies. Together they celebrated Daryl's life and their family in Jesus. Worshiping through pain brought Rebekah's son closer to God than ever before. She clung to the God of eternity and received fresh vision for carrying His love to the nations. There truly is a harvest on the other side of sorrow.

> *Lord, help me run to You in the depths of my pain and release what is too heavy for me to carry. Give me grace, strength, and absolute surrender to reach the other side. When waves of grief crash all around me, remind me that You're by my side.*

- Stay tender and let God carry you through: "I have carried you from birth. I supported you from the moment you left the womb" (Isaiah 46:3).

- Resist anesthetizing your pain. Don't numb yourself with food, TV, alcohol, or busyness. Let God be your Comforter. Walk through all of it, even the most painful parts.

- Refuse isolation. Reach out to friends, even if just to sit in silence with you. Quickly forgive insensitive things people say when trying to bring comfort.

Daryl and Rebekah in Malawi (2011)

Love Your Neighbor

You must love your neighbor
in the same way you love yourself.
MARK 12:31

Amy and David Lancaster are the founding direc-
tors of We Will Go Ministries in Jackson, Mississippi.
Their mission is to help others experience the trans-
forming power of Christ through love and action, but
this calling has not always been easy on them. A man
named Kevin lived in the graveyard across from their
home, and he threatened to kill them nearly every day
for about five years. He had been a cocaine user for
thirty-three years and would sometimes come to their
house in the middle of the night to bang on their door
or windows. He also robbed them and made threats
with guns and knives. Kevin's relentless attacks left
the Lancasters exhausted, feeling like they never had a
moment to simply take a breath.

Thankfully, the Holy Spirit continued to remind them that Kevin was their neighbor, and they needed to love him. Would they be able to love him? Would they be willing to? If they loved God but did not love their neighbors, regardless of who they were, then they were fakes. Love had to look like something, and something is what they did. They made sure to feed and clothe Kevin. Sometimes he would come to prayer meetings and threaten to kill everyone, then join them for food. The Lancasters nevertheless sat in the tension between receiving relentless attacks and showing relentless love—God's love. God was teaching them that even the toughest of cases was still their neighbor.

God longs that all should be saved and have eternal life, so Amy and David's greatest fear was that Kevin would die without knowing Jesus. Amy posted Bible verses around their home and hung a banner in their backyard that had the words of John 10:10: "The thief comes only to steal and kill and destroy; I have come that they may have life, and have it to the full" (NIV). The Word of God is our sword, and Amy stood on His promises as she declared God's Word over Kevin. Kevin came to faith and told Amy and David that they had loved him so fiercely that he couldn't resist this relentless love of Jesus.

We depend on God and on His Word. We don't know who will be saved, healed, and delivered. That is God's knowledge. But we are called to refuse to give up on the promises of God and on our neighbors. No matter what you are going through, refuse to give up. We can't figure everything out on our own. Give Jesus your yes. He says that His yoke is easy, and His burden is light (Matthew 11:30). Jesus cares about the people around you even more than you do, and He will help you love like He does. Ask Jesus to help you to see from His perspective. Put yourself in their situation. Would you want someone to stop for you? Keep reaching out and keep loving.

Lord, You hold everything in Your hands.
Help me love my neighbors and the hungry,
sick, poor, and lost. I trust You with my needs
and theirs. I trust You when life doesn't make
sense. Help me love like You do. I trust You.

- Read the Word: "We have the living Word of God, which is full of energy...It interprets and reveals the true thoughts and secret motives of our hearts" (Hebrews 4:12).

- Filled with the Word, reach out and help someone in need: "When you are generous to the poor, you are enriched with blessings in return" (Proverbs 22:9).

- Surround yourself with positive, loving people who focus on loving God and loving their neighbors.

Amy and Kevin

God's Perfect Timing

There is a divine mystery—a secret surprise that has been
concealed from the world for generations, but now it's
being revealed, unfolded and manifested for every holy
believer to experience.
COLOSSIANS 1:26

While I was on outreach to the village of Chuiba, a
family who had heard testimonies of the blind seeing
asked me to pray for their blind relative, who was also
crippled. I prayed for his eyes and legs, but he showed
no signs of healing. He then asked me to pray for his
headache, and I did. He said his head felt better, and the
entire family came to faith in Jesus. I was encouraged and
discouraged at the same time but asked him to send a
runner to me once he was seeing and walking.

As I was leaving, I heard commotion and yelling.
Some of the villagers were throwing rocks and sand at our
outreach team of international visitors! Our team locked

themselves inside our Land Rover, praying intently. One of my spiritual daughters—adopted into the family of God—called to the blind and the deaf to come for healing prayer. A rock struck me, and pain shot through my back. At that moment I wished she hadn't made such a call since the man with whom I had only just prayed for a few minutes ago wasn't healed. Someone brought a deaf man over to her, and the tiny little girl, full of supernatural boldness, prayed and put her fingers inside his ears. At once he was able to hear. The villagers dropped their rocks!

After some discussion, a group of men wearing intense expressions on their faces called me over. To my shock, they commanded us to build a church for them. Eventually we built two churches and a preschool. We also drilled six water wells. Now they are a strong believing community, and we use this base for spiritual and physical food distribution to thousands of internally displaced people who have since fled to Chuiba.

A few days after the upheaval, I was on our base in the car with a well-to-do friend from another faith. A stranger banged on the window. A little taken aback, I rolled down the window. He had come straight from Chuiba to tell me that the blind, crippled man I had prayed for was now completely healed and working on his farm.

When my friend heard this, he grabbed my hand and placed it over his eyes. He wasn't blind, but he knew he needed spiritual sight. God's timing was phenomenal. The blind man could have been instantly healed, or the runner could have come at any other time. But then I wouldn't have had the opportunity to pray for my friend, who became receptive at that moment. This deepened my understanding of the perfect timing of God.

If you feel discouraged by what isn't happening yet, lean on God's sovereignty. He called all of us to pray for the sick, so we continue to do what He called us to do. We know He is the healer. We pray, we trust, and then we rest in the fact that He is in control. He's in charge. We also remember that heaven is real, so even death has lost its sting.

> *God, give me faith that You will bring to pass what You have in mind. You're in charge of the timing. I trust that I am "completely filled with God as Christ's fullness overflows within [me]."[1]*

---

[1] Colossians 2:10.

- Stand firm, even when your prayers feel ineffectual: "Remember to stay alert and hold firmly to all that you believe. Be mighty and full of courage" (1 Corinthians 16:13).

- Ask and ask like the persistent widow: "God, the true judge, will grant justice to all of his chosen ones who cry out to him night and day" (Luke 18:7).

- Endure: "Yes, this is our God, our great God forever. He will lead us onward until the end, through all time, beyond death, and into eternity!" (Psalm 48:14).

Heidi with a precious, internally displaced mama in Chuiba

Surrender Your Plans

Above all, constantly chase after the realm of God's
kingdom and the righteousness that proceeds from him.
Then all these less important things will be given
to you abundantly.

MATTHEW 6:33

My friend Shapoor Ahmadifar is full of God's love despite having led a challenging life. He fled his home country of Iran for political reasons and was separated from his family. He had lost everything and struggled with intense fear and anxiety for years. Jesus, the Prince of Peace, encountered him and transformed his life when he heard God speak audibly, *Matthew 6:33*, before he ever owned a Bible. While he was still a refugee, his first application for permanent residence in the United Kingdom was denied, so he lost his refugee benefits. He was terrified but realized that he was afraid because he mistakenly put his hope in the government. When he was rejected, feelings of fear, anxiety, and loneliness rose in him. If he were sent back to Iran, he would likely be killed for his faith.

Shapoor began seeking God and reading the Bible for eight hours a day. Even without resources and without knowing where he would live, his greatest prayer was to not lose this precious time. At church, an older English woman asked about his visa application process. After their conversation, she felt compelled to offer him a room in her home. He was so hungry for God that he went on a forty-day fast. He sensed that God wanted him to lose every hope he had in every country and every person on earth. He believed his circumstances would work out for the best once he put all of his hope in God. It was like the passage from his very first encounter: when we seek God first, everything else eventually falls into place.

In that two-year season, he continued to spend about eight hours a day in God's presence and another hour reaching out in ministry. He overcame fear and became a person of hope and joy. He shared the gospel with roughly four hundred people who came to Christ from another faith. The presence of God became so strong when he witnessed that many were healed in body and mind. Before that season, he had aspirations for things like marriage and ministry, but his trials changed him. His heart's cry became, *All I want is Your presence; it is more than enough for me. It is more important than anything else I want.* God broke Shapoor's old self into pieces in the most beautiful way. He let go of his plans and surrendered to God's plan. We are all called to live our lives like that, yielding our plans to God's plans.

My heart's desire is also to be with God where He is. I want His plan, His heart—whatever He says. I don't care where it is. I just want to be with Him. When we live immersed inside His heart, He washes away our fears in His love. We are bent and broken and filled up again with His presence. Are you willing to let go and surrender to Him?

Jesus, I surrender my fears, thoughts, plans, and even my right to know the plans. I yield to You. I lay down the need to figure everything out. Rip away my fear and take me deeper into Your heart, immersed in Your glorious love.

- Seek God: "Nothing brings the soul such sweetness as seeking his living words" (Psalm 19:10).

- Hope in God: "Your perfection and faithfulness are my bodyguards, for you are my hope and I trust in you as my only protection" (Psalm 25:21).

- Surrender your plan: "Lord, direct me throughout my journey so I can experience your plans for my life. Reveal the life-paths that are pleasing to you" (Psalm 25:4).

Shapoor, Meka, and Laura baptizing refugee believers
(face blurred for privacy)

DAY 11

Greater Victory

I live with the confidence that there is nothing in the
universe with the power to separate us from God's love.
I'm convinced that his love will triumph over death,
life's troubles, fallen angels, or dark rulers in the heavens.
There is nothing in our present or future circumstances
that can weaken his love.

ROMANS 8:38

Pastor Pedro Sataca is an Iris pastor and leader in Pemba. In 2011, he was working with Iris in the village of Mieze. Another leader tragically succumbed to a spiritual fall and became poisonously jealous of Pedro and accused him of being a witch doctor. He and several conspirators locked Pedro, his brother, and his neighbor inside Pedro's house, planning to burn them alive. Trapped and facing death, Pedro began to pray. God reminded him that men of God live in prayer. They live in faith, they live in hope, they live in courage, they live in forgiveness, and they live in love.

Outside the house, Pedro heard people saying that Rolland, Pastor Surpresa, and I were coming for a visit. We had felt led to bring our team there although we were unaware of what was going on. A song that we often sing about the Holy Spirit entered Pedro's mind, and he began to worship God. He believed that even if he died in the coming fire, Jesus would receive him in heaven. If Pedro lived, he would live for God. Even facing death, as Romans 8:38 says, nothing can separate us from the love of God:

> He's the hope that holds me and the Stronghold to shelter me, the only God for me, and my great confidence. He will rescue you from every hidden trap of the enemy, and he will protect you from false accusation and any deadly curse. His massive arms are wrapped around you, protecting you. You can run under his covering of majesty and hide. His arms of faithfulness are a shield keeping you from harm. (Psalm 91:2-4)

Because of our unexpected visit, the men who had trapped Pedro became scared and left him alone. The next day in church, I sang the very song God had given Pedro while he was trapped.

Unfortunately, we did not learn the full extent of the situation at the time. The jealous leader had managed to kick Pedro out of local ministry and burn his house. Pedro fled to his farm and lived in a tent for one year. His wife slept in a small hut on the farm. He felt he had lost the central part of his life: his ministry. With no other job, he suffered financially. Like many in Mozambique, he feared he and his wife might starve. He took it as a test from God and determined to persist in prayer. He fasted for ten days and forgave his persecutors, those who had plotted to kill him. He looked to God for new hope and new life.

After that year, another Iris leader called and asked if he would like to attend the Bible School. He accepted with joy. After he graduated, God lifted him up to a new position as pastor. As we wrote this story, we had just finished helping Pastor Pedro build a beautiful new home and guest house for his family. God restores and brings new life!

God, You never leave me or forsake me.
You are just and faithful. I put my hope in You.
I choose to forgive and bless those who have
hurt me. Lord, bring me comfort, new life,
and a greater victory.

- Separate yourself to seek God for new vision: "You are the revelation-light in my darkness, and in your brightness I can see the path ahead" (Psalm 18:28).

- Forgive: "When you are insulted, be quick to forgive and forget it, for you are virtuous when you overlook an offense" (Proverbs 19:11).

- Trust God's timing: "Don't give up; don't be impatient; be entwined as one with the Lord. Be brave and courageous, and never lose hope" (Psalm 27:14).

Pastor Pedro and Liz during disaster relief work on the coastline of Lumwana, where villages were hardest hit by Cyclone Kenneth

All Our Days

Your eyes saw my unformed body;
all the days ordained for me were written in your book
before one of them came to be.
PSALM 139:16 NIV

In 2014, Musy Hart's skin started itching, and one of her ribs kept slipping out of place. She went to several doctors, but they could not give her any answers. Finally, a dermatologist performed an X-ray and found four masses in her lungs—one the size of her fist. She was diagnosed with Hodgkin's Lymphoma stage 4. The news was a complete shock, but she turned to God and remembered Psalm 139. She prayed, *God, I can't add one more day to my life. You have all my days. You know what the outcome is going to be.* As she battled cancer, God took her deeply into the revelation that He has all our days. We do not have ownership over our lives. Our lives belong to Him.

Musy leaned into her relationship with God. She guarded her heart and chose to trust. She decided that no matter what happened, she would not be angry at God. At first, she put great hope in being healed. Then she realized her hope had to be in Jesus. In Him alone do we have eternal life. She received prayer for healing and underwent medical treatments, but she grounded herself in eternity, in Jesus. This United Pursuit lyric spoke to her heart: "Though the seasons change, your love remains."[2] She knew that whether she lived or died, God would remain the same. She would worship Him no matter what.

Musy also realized that she could not get through her battle alone. She needed her loved ones and her community to lift her up. Sometimes, Musy wanted her husband, Will, to be a protector and covering, but she realized that ultimately, she had to rely on God. Will couldn't give her life; only God could. Will fought beside her, but God was her salvation in every moment.

Now Musy is healthy and cancer free. Looking back, she wouldn't trade her experiences for anything because of what God taught her. The fact that life can end in a moment became very real, but this deepened her trust for God. She did not pull back but found that He was the safest place for all her emotions. He gave her peace, supernatural wisdom, and even joy.

---

2   Will Reagan, Brandon Hampton, Michael Ketterer, "Seasons Change," track 7 on *Simple Gospel*, United Pursuit, 2015.

The challenges you endure are not a shock to God. Dive into His presence and into His Word. Worship Him and watch Him fight for you. When you are weak, lean on people who are strong in faith. Many people hide, choosing to go through difficult things alone, but God wants to surround us with the body of Christ. If you are going through a crisis, big or small, share about it with someone close to you. Choose people who will help you bring everything back to God. He is the one you can depend on through it all. Whatever you face, God will give you everything you need as you cling to Him.

God, You know all the days ordained for me.
My life is written in Your Book of Life. I cling
to You today and bring You all my emotions.
Fill me with Your supernatural wisdom, peace,
and joy.

- Don't fight alone. When you feel weak, lean on people who are strong in God. Worship and pray together.

- "Guard the affections of your heart, for they affect all that you are. Pay attention to the welfare of your innermost being, for from there flows the well-spring of life" (Proverbs 4:23).

- Anchor yourself in Jesus: "Before I'd ever seen the light of day, the number of days you planned for me were already recorded in your book" (Psalm 139:16).

The Hart family after Musy's cancer treatments

Lean into Jesus

Because of the crowd, they went up on top of the house and tore away the roof above Jesus' head. And when they had broken through, they lowered the paralyzed man on a stretcher right down in front of him!

Mark 2:4

Yesterday you read about Musy overcoming cancer. Her husband, Will, who is the CEO of Iris Global, also has a story to share. In his words, "I may not have had the physical pain, but I 100 percent walked through cancer." When Will first heard the word *cancer*, countless thoughts raced through his mind. The uncertainty of Musy's prognosis was torture, and his greatest fear was that their three children might grow up without their mom. He wanted next steps. He wanted a plan.

Will and Musy faced a difficult choice in how they would respond, and they only had one opportunity to face their crisis with faith. They made an intentional decision, right from the start, to trust Jesus in everything. That is how they live their lives. They lean into His voice. They understand that our own strategies and plans are not the answer; Jesus is the answer. They also listened to doctors and completed all of the recommended treatments. God gives us brilliant minds *and* medical solutions *and* supernatural miracles. There are many ways to be healed, but Jesus is the healer.

When someone close to us goes through a trial, we do too. And it is incredibly painful to watch a loved one suffer. We want to be strong, but sometimes we may feel helpless or afraid of losing them. My husband, Rolland, had cerebral malaria and post-traumatic stress disorder. For nearly two years he was severely debilitated and lost his short-term memory. We felt like we had lost him. Thankfully, through rest, anointed doctors, and much prayer, Jesus healed Rolland completely.

The way we live, especially during seasons of challenge, can bring God glory. What we need to remember is that we don't have to be strong all of the time; it's completely normal to feel sad, depressed, angry, or confused. Struggling does not mean that we lack faith either. In fact, our faith often grows when we struggle with Jesus. He cares about our hearts. He can handle every emotion and every question, so go to Him in the midst of it all.

Be honest with friends too. Whether you or your loved one is suffering, choose a few people with whom you are close to who will support you as you overcome with Jesus. You don't have to take everyone's advice or invite everyone on the journey. Simply listen to people who love God and love you. If you are walking with someone through a trial, try to help them encounter the Lord during their time of difficulty. Like the four friends in Mark 2 who pressed past the crowds and broke through the rooftop to deliver their friend to Jesus, be tenacious in your pursuit of Him. Pray together. Ask God questions. Lean into His voice and His Word. His grace is sufficient for you.

God, my circumstances are bigger than I can handle alone, but I choose to lean into Your all-sufficient grace today. I step into Your heart and Your love. I come into the secret place again leaning on my beloved.

- Remember that "every detail of our lives is continually woven together to fit into God's perfect plan of bringing good into our lives" (Romans 8:28).

- Seek wisdom from God and medical professionals: "Your whispers in the night give me wisdom, showing me what to do next" (Psalm 16:7).

- Process and pray: "Whenever trouble strikes, I will keep crying out to you, for I know your help is on the way" (Psalm 86:7).

The Hart Family (2020)

Never Give Up

I'm trained in the secret of overcoming all things,
whether in fullness or in hunger. And I find that the
strength of Christ's explosive power infuses me
to conquer every difficulty.

PHILIPPIANS 4:12–13

Today's story began in the ocean near our home in Pemba, Mozambique. I was snorkeling far out in the water with colorful fish and coral below me, thinking about how different the world looks underwater. My next thought was how the kingdom of God brings us a similarly different perspective. At once God spoke clearly to my spirit: *I want you to build a university.* I was so shocked that I sucked water into my snorkel. I thought, *Who, me?*

Even though I had studied for ten years and had already earned my doctorate, I couldn't imagine God using me to start a university. And yet I sensed God wanted me to begin right away. I changed clothes and went straight to our Village of Joy base. I drew a big circle around a baobab tree with a stick and said, "Who wants to go to school? We are starting first grade right now." Year by year we built new classrooms, first out of bamboo, then concrete blocks. Now we have one of the best primary/secondary schools in the nation, with nearly 3,700 students.

Some people hear prophetic words and think they're going to happen overnight. They think there's little or no effort involved, but the Lord calls us to work with Him. He will put something in your heart, but He expects you, as an obedient son or daughter, to do what He has asked. Start there. Don't be afraid of hard work, and don't be afraid to study to show yourself approved (2 Timothy 2:15).

An incredible amount of hard work was put into earning a doctorate degree. A massive amount of hard work was behind our last fifteen years building Iris University. We were told we would never secure the appropriate land use permits. That alone took seven years and countless hours of work. We had to pay high taxes. We needed construction, professors, security, and accreditation. We needed to build a brand-new two-lane road. Every single element brought challenges with it and took significantly longer than expected. We failed our first defense for accreditation. We had to get better. Finally, we were able to commence our first classes at Iris University, fully accredited, in 2021.

In Mozambique, we face war and terrorism. One of our biggest fears has been that radical insurgents might burn down our university. We could have given up at any step of the way. No matter how challenging things may be, never give up. Try again. If we don't quit, we win. We must fix our eyes on Jesus. I remain hopeful by looking into the faces of the young men and women in the villages and on my team. I see their hope. I see destiny. They believe that one day they will be able to study at Iris University. I remember the promises of God for them and for me, and I take courage.

God, show me the next step to take as I partner with You in the dreams You have put on my heart. Give me courage and perseverance. I know I can do all things through Christ who strengthens me.

- Don't give up: "Patient endurance will refine our character, and proven character leads us back to hope" (Romans 5:4).

- "Look away from the natural realm and fasten [your] gaze onto Jesus who birthed faith within us and who leads us forward into faith's perfection" (Hebrews 12:2).

- Don't take short cuts. Always walk in integrity and don't be afraid of hard work: "Study to [show yourself] approved unto God" (2 Timothy 2:15 KJV).

Heidi and children from Maringanha village looking at the architectural design plans for Iris University

Trust in God

At the very moment I called out to you, you answered me!
You strengthened me deep within my soul
and breathed fresh courage into me.
PSALM 138:3

When those close to us are going through their hardest moments, it is a privilege to stand with them in prayer. Several of my spiritual daughters have experienced difficult births. Others have watched their babies fight to stay alive. I feel like a lioness when I contend for mothers and babies in prayer. A special type of urgency rises up within me.

One of my dearest friends, Rebekah, faced a critical medical emergency with her grandson, Ezra. Ezra was just ten days old when he was rushed to the ER for a life-threatening problem with his intestines and bowels, which had been twisting and untwisting—likely since birth. The twists had begun to cut off blood circulation.

Doctors hurried him to the operating room immediately, prepping in the elevator. After a successful emergency surgery, the doctors said Ezra had been perhaps two hours away from death. If the ER staff had delayed treatment even a little, he would have lost his bowels and possibly died. But he didn't. He was saved just in time and experienced the power of prayer and medical intervention.

For Ezra's mother, two realities were hardest to endure. The first was having to watch her son suffer extreme pain. It was especially terrible not being able to hold him, nurse him, or bring any kind of comfort to him. The second toughest reality for her to face was that the world outside simply carried on while hers fell apart. The earth did not stand still, anxiously holding its breath over her son's life in limbo. After having already lost a son in a miscarriage, Ezra's mother could hardly bear the thought of losing another baby, but she remained hopeful through the power of prayer.

God spoke to Ezra's mother about trusting Him, assuring her that He is always good. She had faith that her son would live, and she also believed that if Ezra died, then he would be with God, who wanted him from the beginning of time. Still, the experience was so difficult at times that simply whispering, "Just trust," regardless of whether she felt it or not, was all that she could manage. If she did not trust God or at least try her best to do so, then she would surely panic and crumble. She gathered people around her in prayer—Rebekah and me included—and we fought together. Having friends and family with you during a trial gives you strength to endure.

Keep your heart open to God and listen to what He tells you. He is bigger than every situation. He speaks and moves in the midst of chaos. Ask Him to give you words to stand on. He gave Ezra's mother the strength to keep going and keep trusting, and after several more medical emergencies, we all thank God that Ezra is now a healthy, joyful, growing boy. We pray his story will bring hope and courage to others in situations like these.

God, help me live my life with unshakable confidence no matter what happens. I choose to trust You and put my hope in You. Thank You that You respond to my prayers and give me strength to endure.

- Take time to listen to your feelings and emotions. Write them down and process them with God and people you trust. Then give those feelings and emotions to God.

- Remember his goodness: "So why would I fear the future? For your goodness and love pursue me all the days of my life" (Psalm 23:6).

- Trust: "You are my strength and my shield from every danger. When I fully trust in you, help is on the way" (Psalm 28:7).

Ezra (2020)

Stop for the One

*Jesus put his hands over the man's eyes a second time
and made him look up. The man opened his eyes wide
and he could see everything perfectly. His eyesight
was completely restored!*

Mark 8:25

One of my greatest joys is visiting friends and meeting new people in the villages of Cabo Delgado. One day we were dedicating a new home for my dear friend Tina, who is now in heaven. As I walked down steep, winding dirt paths toward my truck, I noticed a woman sitting out under the full sun. Mozambique is so hot that almost no one ever wants sits out of the shade. I wondered why she was there. I sensed God wanted me to stop, but I was already late for my discipleship meeting. It's embarrassing to admit this, but I told God I was running late and looked at my watch.

I quickly remembered that if the Lord leads you to stop, you should stop. So, I went over and found that the woman was blind. Using the local dialect, I asked her name. She replied that she had no name. *How could that be?* I thought. Perhaps she didn't understand the question. I asked again in Portuguese, the national language. Again, she told me she had no name. How could she have no name or no friends around? Another woman sat across the way, so I asked her the same question. She said, "She's blind. She doesn't have a name."

I held the blind woman's hands and asked if I could give her a name. She grinned, revealing her few remaining teeth. God gave me the name *Uthelia*, which means, "you exist with joy." I told her that God saw her and that she existed with joy. Now she had a name, and she broke into laughter. It was beautiful. As I prayed, Jesus opened her eyes. I watched them turn from cloudy white to brown. I was completely undone. She looked at me, and I asked her if she wanted to know the One who opened her eyes. I told her about Jesus. He would love her and forgive her sins and take care of her. Immediately she received the Lord. It was easy because her heart was so open. I asked the woman nearby to call Uthelia by her new name. They became friends, laughing together with this wonderful joy.

That day I learned again about stopping for the One and allowing the Lord to rule over my schedule. That was a huge lesson for me. My greatest challenge was obeying and stopping when I felt like I had something more important to do. Some of my team members lead hundreds of churches, and I wanted to honor their time. I know it is important to show up on time for work and for commitments, but there are also times when the Lord wants to interrupt your schedule, and it's not always convenient. When you allow the Holy Spirit to speak to you, sometimes He will ask you to put aside what you might consider important. He is asking you to stop for the One.

God, I give You my schedule. Help me to be so yielded to You that I won't be led by my own understanding but by Your Spirit, empowered to stop for the one in need.

- Ask God to "illuminate the eyes of your imagination, flooding you with light, until you experience the full revelation of the hope of his calling" (Ephesians 1:18).

- "Give God the right to direct your life [and schedule], and as you trust him along the way you'll find he pulled it off perfectly!" (Psalm 37:5).

- Keep your eyes and heart open as you believe that God will show you who to stop for each day.

Heidi making new friends in a village of Cabo Delgado

Beauty for Ashes

Keep your thoughts continually fixed on all that is authentic and real, honorable and admirable, beautiful and respectful, pure and holy, merciful and kind. And fasten your thoughts on every glorious work of God, praising him always.

PHILIPPIANS 4:8

Lynn Eldridge was raised going to church on Sundays, but during the week, her home was not a safe place. Her mother was verbally and physically abusive, and Lynn came to suffer from severe depression and bipolar disorder. As a teenager, she closed her heart to God and her mom, finding herself in a relationship with a drug dealer at school. By age seventeen, she was addicted to cocaine, and older men used her to transport money and drugs. The FBI uncovered the drug cartel, but since Lynn was underage, she was not sent to prison. Her mother drove her directly to the last place anyone would ever find her:

Bible college. The moment she arrived on campus, she started crying. At once she decided to follow Jesus and found herself free from addiction, anorexia, depression, and bipolar disorder.

Unfortunately, Lynn eventually fell back into her old patterns, and for several decades, her life spiraled downward. At her lowest point, she went on a cocaine binge and overdosed. She thought she was going to die and cried out to God for help. Her phone rang. It was a girl from junior high whom Lynn hadn't seen in years. "It might sound crazy," the girl said, "but God told me to call you." Stunned, Lynn checked herself into a rehab center. Desperate and mentally tormented, she searched for peace through many religions and practices. One day, she was suicidal and called her cousin in a panic. He convinced her to come to a healing meeting at church. The speaker did not know Lynn but told her that he sensed she had struggled with addiction and depression since childhood and that God wanted to set her free. She ran to the altar in tears. Then she began attending the church's healing rooms and found a professional counselor.

Lynn's healing came through a long, arduous journey of gradually discovering who God is and who she is in Christ. Reading about Jesus healing the mentally tormented gave her hope for her own healing. Forgiveness was a major key to her freedom as well. She wanted to live without offense and follow God's ways. A friend helped her realize that she had grown up believing God was angry and critical and that she was never good enough. That was her perspective, but it was far from God's truth.

Through prayer and Scriptures, Lynn saw for herself that God is a loving Father, and that made all the difference. She wrote Bible verses on note cards, meditating on God's Word daily. She filled her home with worship, especially songs about identity. Through this process, God gave her beauty from ashes, and Jesus became her best friend. God also put a deep desire in Lynn to invite others into freedom. She wants everyone to know that if Jesus healed her, then He can heal them too. Lynn is proof that the power and love of God can transform any life and that healing is available to everyone who follows Him.

God, You are a loving father. You have
forgiven my unrighteousness by the love,
power, and willing sacrifice of Jesus. Help me
walk in the freedom Jesus paid for on the cross
and in my true identity in Christ.

- Define God biblically, not on self-conclusions, criticisms, or how others treat you: "You truly are my Father, my only God, and my strong deliverer!" (Psalm 89:26).

- Find out who you are from God's Word. Meditate on verses about your identity. Fill your home with worship that brings God's presence and truth.

- Follow Jesus, not your thoughts and feelings or those of others: "What delight comes to the one who follows God's ways!" (Psalm 1:1).

Lynn (2020)

Be Still and Know

When you sit enthroned under the shadow of Shaddai,
you are hidden in the strength of God Most High.
PSALM 91:1

In April of 2018, Jason Lee Jones was diagnosed with stage 4B throat cancer. For context, there is no stage five. His ear, nose, and throat specialist cried while telling him to cancel all future commitments. Within a week, the lead cancer specialist prescribed thirty-five radiation treatments and six chemo treatments. His wife, Gina, noted that doctors only cry when they doubt their patients will survive.

Months before this fateful appointment, while ministering with us in Mozambique, Jason heard God tell him that He wanted to teach Jason a realm of stillness he had never known before. Back in the doctor's office, Jason thought of Psalm 46:10: "Be still, and know that I am God" (NIV). As soon as I learned of his diagnosis, I called him. We prayed Psalm 91, which became a constant declaration throughout his struggle. He refused to be consumed with questions of why he had gotten cancer or why he hadn't been supernaturally healed. His biggest concern was how to support his family since he couldn't lead worship or work. God simply reminded him to be still. Many people supported his family with prayer and finances, showing kindness far beyond their expectations.

In stillness Jason learned a facet of God that he'd never known before: the fruit of the Holy Spirit is the highest form of spiritual warfare. Jason was determined to fight with patience, outlasting his enemies. Whenever he lost his sense of peace, he reminded himself that he was seated in the shadow of God Most High. He hid himself in the promises of God's Word, face-to-face with Jesus. During radiation treatments, he declared Isaiah 60:5: "You will look and be radiant, your heart will throb and swell with joy" (NIV). He prayed, *God, the physicians are treating me with radiation, but You are the radiance. You surround me. I look to You, and I am radiant.* On his sickest days, he felt like he was swallowing razor blades, and he would lay on the couch and listen to worship music. Whenever he felt anxious or frustrated, he remembered that those feelings are not fruits of the Spirit, and he refocused his heart. Jason completed treatment in June of 2018. By September of that same year, he received the results of the PET scan: he was cancer free! God brought him to the other side.

In 2 Corinthians 3, Paul teaches us that we become what we behold. The idea is that when we stand before God and minister to Him, He reveals Himself to us, and we reflect His character. Like King David, it is normal to ask questions and experience emotions. David was raw and real in the Psalms but always brought his concerns to God. Imagine yourself with Abba Father, with His massive arms wrapped around you, covered by His majesty. Bring your burdens to Him. He will meet you with love and faithfulness. And remember that you are seated under the shadow of El Shaddai, God Most High.

I posture myself under the shadow of Shaddai,
God Most High. I live in the stillness of God,
face-to-face with Jesus. I become what I
behold. God, You're the hope that holds me
and the stronghold to shelter me. I am hidden
in Your promises.

- Be still. Posture yourself under the shadow of Shaddai in a place of stillness: "His massive arms are wrapped around you, protecting you" (Psalm 91:4).

- Behold Jesus: "For no matter what, I will still sing with praise, for living before his face is my saving grace!" (Psalm 42:5).

- You become what you behold. The fruit of the Spirit will grow in you as you sit still in God's presence, beholding His face.

Jason and his family

Let Your Light Shine

Your lives are like salt among the people...
Your lives light up the world.
MATTHEW 5:13-14

I longed to reach the unreached people of Londo, a village across the bay, but we needed a boat. A generous donor purchased one for us, but my team said it was impossible to get it to Pemba. I saw other boats around, so I knew it had to be possible. Every time someone told me that it could not be done, I persevered because I felt the Lord's heart for the people of Londo and other nearby islands who had never heard the name of Jesus. Still, reaching that village would prove anything but easy.

A year after our boat had been purchased, we finally got it to Pemba using a giant truck and a trailer. We still needed a dingy to carry us to shores that lacked docks and a captain who spoke the local languages. Again, people told us this wasn't possible. I believed God anyway.

After several months, our dingy arrived, and we found a captain. On our first journey, we hit giant waves that made our whole team miserably seasick. Everyone was throwing up violently, and we had to turn back. We felt completely, utterly defeated. As soon as we crawled to shore, many members of our team said they would never board a boat again. When I prayed, the word *Dramamine* came to mind. You might laugh, but seasickness pills, which had to be brought in from outside the country, were vital to getting us back on that boat.

Our next voyage made it to Londo. Many children welcomed us, curious to meet the rare visitors who had come to their village. We met with a village leader and other important men. We told them how difficult it had been to reach them, and we shared about Jesus and how He gave His life because He loved them. We also brought a solar audio Bible recorded in their native language, and their faces lit up with extraordinary joy. They had never heard the gospel before. Many came to faith. Sadly, on the way home, one of our engines blew up. It took months to receive replacement parts from Canada. But when we finally made it back to Londo, the villagers lined up along the shore, quoting the New Testament in Makua and singing songs from the solar audio Bible. It was one of the most joyful days of my life.

Some people will tell you that your dream is impossible, but if your dream comes from God, He will help you find a way. It took many people to reach Londo with the gospel. It required boat builders, engine repairmen, Bible translators who spent twenty years translating the New Testament into Makua, teams bringing parts, a captain, and logistics teams. God uses many parts of His body and all their gifts together. His greatest blessings are expressed in community. Whether bringing boat parts through the airport or driving the boat to Pemba, each person played an important role and shared their talents. God longs for the lost, and He puts great hope inside our hearts. That hope gives us courage to travel difficult roads or seas.

God, help me share my story. Whatever I do, wherever I go, let me be salt and light. Let me shine for You. Give me your heart for people who do not know Jesus and give me courage to reach them.

- Listen to the Holy Spirit for the solution, especially when your challenge feels impossible: "We must live in the Holy Spirit and follow after him" (Galatians 5:25).

- Work together as the body of Christ: "God has carefully designed each member and placed it in the body to function as he desires" (1 Corinthians 12:18).

- Share your story. Every believer is called: "How can they hear the message of life if there is no one there to proclaim it?" (Romans 10:14).

Heidi ministering on Jimpia Island near Londo

God of All Comfort

Sarah's faith embraced the miracle power to conceive
even though she was barren and was past the age
of childbearing, for the authority of her faith rested
in the One who made the promise, and she tapped
into his faithfulness.

HEBREWS 11:11

My dear friends Chuck and Sally Cook wed when
Sally was 38. They longed to have children, but after two
unsuccessful pregnancies, doctors said it was unlikely.
After Sally's first miscarriage, her mind spun in circles
wondering why it had happened. Her second miscarriage
occurred right after her father's funeral. She and Chuck
were devastated. Sally believes her first two babies are in
heaven, but losing them was still deeply painful. Still, the
story of Abraham and Sarah felt like a promise straight
from God to their hearts. They believed He would
give them a child, and on the plane ride home from

Mozambique, God met them powerfully. He showed them that their perspective was distorted by grief.

Chuck and Sally took careful stock of what they believed about God, themselves, and their situation. They didn't know all the answers, but they held to the truth: God is a good Father, and He is for us. When Sally got pregnant for the third time, she was overjoyed. They had one terrifying moment when she started bleeding again. She prayed in the Spirit, refusing to believe it was another miscarriage. She and Chuck stayed up most of the night, interceding. It felt like a spiritual battle between life and death. God gave Sally an impression of an angel reading a thick book—the Book of Life for her son. Not a book of weeks but of years and years. Grace and peace superseded fear, and the rest of her pregnancy went smoothly. Josiah was born beautiful and strong. Now he is a healthy, energetic boy, full of life.

When we suffer, it can be a challenge to maintain our belief that God is for us and will help us overcome. We may wonder if we did something wrong or if we are being punished. And our past can make us fearful about the future, expecting another heartbreak. If you've suffered loss, let grief be what it needs to be. Psalm 34:18 says, "The Lord is close to all whose hearts are crushed by pain." Being honest with God opens your heart to receive His tender care. If you are disappointed or feel He has let you down, tell Him. He wants to meet you in the middle of it all. If you feel stuck, reach out to friends or professional counselors to walk with you in the process.

Today we are ministering to many displaced people in Mozambique. They have lost homes, livelihoods, and family members. I hold them in my arms and pray for comfort to wash over them. I will never have every answer, but I know God "heals the wounds of every shattered heart" (Psalm 147:3). God wants to comfort us as we mourn, and intimacy with Him—hearing His voice—renews our hope.

Lord, even when Your path takes me through the valley of deepest darkness, fear will never conquer me, for You already have! You remain close to me and lead me through it all the way. Your authority is my strength and my peace.

- Get into the presence of God and get His perspective. Allow God's wrap-around presence to protect you as your champion defender (Psalm 62:6).

- Get help. Talk to someone, whether it is a friend or a professional counselor.

- "Tell him all your troubles and pour out your heart-longings to him. Believe me when I tell you—he will help you!" (Psalm 62:8).

Chuck, Sally, and Josiah

Overcome Together

Hear me, Lord, and answer me, for I am poor and needy.
Guard my life, for I am faithful to you; save your servant
who trusts in you. You are my God.
PSALM 86:1–2 NIV

The Mozambique government provides Iris Global with a list of names of internally displaced people (IDPs) in need of food kits, and we utilize these lists during our spiritual and physical food distributions. It was during one of these distributions in Cabo Delgado that I came to meet a special woman named Amina. Amina had walked approximately five kilometers (or 3.1 miles) to reach our distribution point, hoping and praying to obtain food for her family, who had nothing left. But Amina's name was not on the list. Still, when I saw her, it was as if the Holy Spirit tapped me on the shoulder so that I would stop and listen to her story.

Al Shabaab, a terrorist group, had burned down Amina's home and forced her to watch her husband's beheading. Then they crucified his body and forced their relatives and neighbors to bathe in his blood. As they often do, the terrorists intentionally left a few people alive, including Amina, to tell others about the group's atrocities and spread terror. Amina fled to nearby Pemba with her baby. Along the way, she met a young, orphaned girl named Maria, who was eleven years old, and welcomed her into her family.

Amina's kindness and generosity left me completely undone. Here was a woman who had just lost everything and suffered unimaginable horrors, but when she saw someone else in need, she chose compassion. This is true Christianity and true love: "Religion that God our Father accepts as pure and faultless is this: to look after orphans and widows in their distress and to keep oneself from being polluted by the world" (James 1:27 NIV). After listening to Amina's story, I felt compelled to visit her home. She never could have managed to carry the food such a long distance, so we loaded a heavy food kit onto a truck and drove to her hut.

As the truck slowed and pulled up to Amina's hut, all of us started to cry. Proudly displayed in front of her home stood a tall, wooden cross. It was a bold statement and symbol to the world that she would never deny Jesus, no matter the circumstances: "Blessed are those who are persecuted because of righteousness, for theirs is the kingdom of heaven" (Matthew 5:10 NIV). We prayed together and gifted her a solar audio Bible in her language. We also helped her secure the necessary documentation for Maria to attend school. Amina's life is a testimony that has personally moved me to pursue an even greater depth of Christ-like love and to trust completely in Jesus, who will lead us to safety through even the most unthinkable trials.

Although it can be tempting to sulk in suffering and adopt a victim mentality, the Lord wants us to go beyond the place of victimhood to see the beauty in caring for someone else. I believe God brought Amina and Maria together to save and support each other through horrific tragedy. He created us to reach out and find comfort in one another, so reach out to someone even in the midst of pain. As you do, the Lord will deeply and miraculously comfort your heart. We overcome together.

God, thank You that You created me for connection with others. I am not alone, and I am not a victim. Show me who to stop for today and with whom You want me to overcome.

- Cry out to God: "Whenever trouble strikes, I will keep crying out to you, for I know your help is on the way" (Psalm 86:7).

- Comfort others: "The Lord has anointed me to proclaim good news to the poor. He has sent me to bind up the brokenhearted, to proclaim freedom for the captives" (Isaiah 61:1 NIV).

- Embrace trials: "Rejoice and be glad, because great is your reward in heaven, for in the same way they persecuted the prophets who were before you" (Matthew 5:12 NIV).

The inspiring cross in front of Amina's hut

DAY 22

Omniscient and Omnipotent

Delight yourself in the Lord,
and he will give you the desires of your heart.
PSALM 37:4 ESV

As someone who has been ministering cross-cultur-ally in poor, destitute areas for decades, it was difficult for me to receive personal blessings for a long time. This difficulty was also connected to a traumatic childhood experience when I was twelve years old. I had asked my mother for a horse, and let's just say the conversation did not go well for me. I vowed to myself that I would never ask anyone for anything ever again. Through prayer and counseling as an adult, I realized I had never fully for-given my mother for that incident. I was finally able to do so by the power of the Holy Spirit.

Years later, I was speaking at a conference in Red Deer, Canada, when the pastor told me that cowboys were waiting outside and asking for me. It seemed strange for many reasons, especially since I was ministering, but the pastor insisted. Sure enough, I walked outside to find two cowboys and a cowgirl wearing jeans with big belt buckles, hats, and boots. Father God had told them that I once asked Him for a big, black horse, and He never forgets. This experience was not a vision; before my very eyes stood a majestic, black horse named Baby that these cowboys had sacrificed to purchase and transport all the way from Montana to Canada—for me!

Mind you, I hadn't told a soul that I had prayed for a horse except my sister. I will never forget jumping onto that beautiful horse and galloping across the parking lot and into the fields. My hands lifted toward the sky, and tears streamed from my eyes. Everything shifted for me that day. I truly felt the love of the Father as he spoke to my heart that this horse was a sign for me to receive deeply of his love.

Another sign of God's love came to me in the form of a photograph. The cowboys had taken a picture of Baby and me galloping through the golden fields of harvest, but for some reason the film was double exposed. When the pictures were developed, an image of a conference at our Iris Malawi base, where we were feeding tens of thousands of people and witnessing miraculous healings, appeared on top of the image of Baby and me. The Lord spoke to my heart and told me to share with the church that this was the time of harvest.

As believers in Jesus, we have an incredible privilege in gifting forgiveness to others, even those whom we might feel have not necessarily earned it. When we forgive others, God heals our hearts, and we can run into His arms and receive His blessings. Once I had forgiven my mother, God released me from my childhood vow that I would never ask anyone for anything. It is okay to ask God for personal blessings. He is big enough to grant our personal desires without minimizing His love and care for the dying, desperate, broken, and needy people of the world. He is omniscient and omnipotent, and He never, ever forgets our prayers.

Father, let me rest in Your love, let me rest in Your loving arms. Show me Your goodness and grace. Teach me more about Your nature. Lord Jesus, I release a gift of forgiveness to anyone who has every hurt me. Thank You, Jesus.

- Forgive: "When you pray, make sure you forgive the faults of others so that your Father in heaven will also forgive you" (Matthew 6:14).

- Experience Father God's love: "The same way a loving father feels toward his children—that's but a sample of your tender feelings toward us, your beloved children, who live in awe of you" (Psalm 103:13).

- Receive: "Every gift God freely gives us is good and perfect, streaming down from the Father of lights" (James 1:17).

Heidi riding Baby, who lives in Montana and works with people with disabilities and emotional trauma

Eyes to See

*I pray that the eyes of your heart may be enlightened
in order that you may know the hope to which he has
called you, the riches of his glorious inheritance
in his holy people.*

EPHESIANS 1:18 NIV

Earlier I shared the story of Uthelia and how she met Jesus when He healed her eyesight and gave her a name. Maybe you wondered what stopping for the one might look like in your life. Stopping for the one means loving someone in a tangible way, big or small. Most of us lead busy lives trying to accommodate full schedules, which makes it challenging to pause or slow down. I've found it incredibly helpful to add flex time to my schedule. That way, I'm not always in a rush. I also ask God to open the eyes of my heart so that I can see what He sees. This proved invaluable when I met a courageous woman named Eliza.

Eliza had lost her father, husband, and sister when radical insurgents entered her village. She and her mother had been working on the family farm and returned home to find that the insurgents had taken her father, the secretary of the city. The insurgents burned down the church and beheaded Eliza's husband, the local pastor. His family could not find his head and could only bury his body. Eliza fled with her children and her mother, having witnessed evil beyond comprehension. She shook and sobbed as she shared her story with us, telling us she that had been living in a mud hut with nineteen people ever since and that her children slept on the dirt floor. I held her in my arms and wept without saying a word. Naturally, we helped Eliza with her living situation, but what she needed most was someone to stop for her, to comfort her and to listen.

Human suffering around the world is overwhelming. If we dwell only on our suffering, it's easy to lose all hope. However, as the body of Christ, we are empowered by the Spirit of God. We are the first responders who live from the secret place. We are the feet on the ground, so when I sit with a traumatized person, I ask the Lord to allow me to feel whatever he or she may feel in their moment of sharing. I ask the Holy Spirit to come and personally comfort the one who is mourning. Sometimes, as was the case with Eliza, there are no words. But as we seek the heart of God in the midst of pressure or persecution, He will eventually quiet our hearts. Mercy and compassion may flow again through our little lives laid down.

God will help you see and stop for people. This might look like giving food to a homeless person or buying groceries for an elderly neighbor. It could be smiling at someone in a grocery store or coffee shop. For all you know, that person might be incredibly lonely. It's easy to overlook these people, but they might be desperate for someone to say hello or stop to have a coffee with them. Uthelia was most impacted by identity; Father God saw her and gave her a name. Make room in your schedule, keep your eyes peeled, and open your heart. As your eyes open, you might see things you would have otherwise missed if you simply went about your business, doing your own thing. People long to be seen and loved. This is what it means to stop for the one.

God, give me eyes to see what You see and a heart to feel what You feel so that I stop for the one. Help me live from the secret place inside Your heart and carry Your love and comfort to those in need.

- Pray for eyes to see: "Lovers of God have been given eyes to see with spiritual discernment and ears to hear from God" (Proverbs 20:12).

- Add flex time to your schedule so that you can stop. Don't be intimidated by how small a gesture feels. The simplest things can touch people's hearts deeply.

- Slow down, contemplate, and abide in him: "Your life will be fruitless unless you live your life intimately joined to mine" (John 15:4).

Eliza with her family and those living together
in a one-room home

This Too Shall Pass

*We are convinced that every detail of our lives is
continually woven together to fit into God's perfect plan of
bringing good into our lives, for we are his lovers who have
been called to fulfill his designed purpose.*

ROMANS 8:28

My dear friends Jeff and Gena Barney owned a stunning home in California, but during the fierce Lilac Fire of 2017, it burned to the ground. They were in Alaska when the fire happened, and friends sent a video of their house ablaze. They lost everything: clothes, furniture, family photo albums, cars, one-of-a-kind surfboards . . . everything. They had collected many unique, beautiful works of art over the years, and the loss struck near their hearts. They saw a blob of melted silver and wondered if it was their cutlery. Not even a cup could be found amid the ashes. It was all so surreal that their minds couldn't comprehend the devastation. They thought, *This can't be happening!*

Years later they would find themselves looking for special items or important documents before remembering that all of it had been lost to the flames. They reminded themselves that it was just stuff, but that stuff had been meaningful. They grieved for the memories and keepsakes of their old life. They worried their fire insurance company would refuse to compensate them for the losses, but the opposite happened. The company was extremely supportive and provided everything they needed—even beyond their expectations. Jeff, a custom home builder, built a beautiful new home. They marveled at how God smoothed the path ahead of them.

Bad things happen to good people, and we often don't understand why. But God is not surprised by your situation. He knows everything you will go through in life. It doesn't help to question Him; instead, read His Word and pray His Word. Find comfort in the Scriptures. During times of devastation, look at other aspects of your life and have a thankful heart. Even when it feels like absolutely everything is lost, God is right there with us. He's *still* got this and remains in control. He will go before you and stick closer than a brother (Proverbs 18:24 NIV). Each trial will pass one day, although it may seem impossible to believe. You are His child, and you can trust Him. Have patience and endurance while He works things out. Keep trusting, keep waiting, and watch how God will turn all things around for your good.

*God, when I can't see the solution, help
me trust You. You are not surprised by my
situation. You love me, and I am in Your hands.
Connect me to Your heart and nourish me with
Your love. Show me the ways You are working
all things for my good. Give me patience and
endurance. Thank You that You are faithful.*

- Be still: "I am standing in absolute stillness, silent before the one I love, waiting as long as it takes for him to rescue me" (Psalm 62:5).

- Listen to God's voice through His Word: "For every word God speaks is sure and every promise pure" (Psalm 12:6).

- Reach out to someone you trust to talk to and pray with about your situation.

Jeff and Gena

Catch the Wind

Each test is an opportunity to trust him more, for along with every trial God has provided for you a way of escape that will bring you out of it victoriously.

1 CORINTHIANS 10:13

After the victory of reaching Londo, we were excited when we were ready to visit again. As we crossed the bay, cyclone winds whipped up, blowing water sideways and flooding our boat. Determined, a small team and I used the dingy to reach the shore. We were soaking wet and shivering, but our new friends from the village built us a fire. We remembered the shipwreck of the apostle Paul and prayed quietly that no snakes would jump out of the fire to bite us. We contacted our captain, who was still struggling to save the flooded boat. Sadly, he explained that it was not salvageable. Another captain, who happened to be drunk, responded to our emergency flare and rescued those remaining on the boat.

We slept in a mud hut that the villagers had built for us as a gift, and although grateful to our hosts, we had a rough night of broken flashlights, dead cell phones, and fire ants. None of us slept more than a couple of hours.

The villagers woke us before dawn, extremely excited for us to dedicate their new church. Though exhausted, we found great joy in sharing the gospel and worshiping with our new brothers and sisters. I was supposed to depart the next day for a speaking engagement in Oxford, so we had to find a way home to Pemba without our vessel. Someone lent us a small wooden boat to check our half-sunken vessel for supplies. Taking what we could, we decided to use our rubber dingy to attempt to cross the bay. It filled with water, nearly sinking us, and we paid an exorbitant price to catch a ride on an old bird-poop-covered fishing boat that happened to pass by. Soon after, its engine blew up. Surging waves threatened to smash us against black rocks. Finally, six nearly naked fishermen passed in yet another boat and took pity on us. Not wanting us to feel uncomfortable with their lack of clothing, one swam to shore through huge swells to grab shorts for the crew. They set sail, and we caught the wind. We made it home!

We feared for our lives many times that day, but I held on to hope by remembering the promises of God over my life about Mozambique, Iris University, and the world. Since all of them were not yet fulfilled, I believed we had to make it to the other side, and we did. We also led those six fishermen to the Lord and gifted the captain a New Testament.

Just like our boat needed to catch the wind, we, too, need to position ourselves to catch the wind of the Holy Spirit. He can bring us to places that would be impossible to reach without His power, and He provides a way to bring you out of trouble. It may not come in the way you expect; you never know who or what the Lord may send to rescue you. Ask the Lord how He wants you to minister to those He sends your way.

Lord, I trust You in this wild storm. You will get me to the other side. I trust You for every promise You have spoken over me. What You have said, You will bring to pass.

- Learn and pray the Word. Use "the mighty razor-sharp Spirit-sword of the spoken Word of God" to fight through storms (Ephesians 6:17–18).

- Be inspired by biblical heroes: "We see our difficulties as the substance that produces for us an eternal, weighty glory far beyond all comparison" (2 Corinthians 4:17).

- Catch the wind. Constantly live positioned to catch the wind of the Holy Spirit and let Him take you to your destination.

Heidi and crew near Londo

God Speaks in Grief

You make known to me the path of life;
you will fill me with joy in your presence,
with eternal pleasures at your right hand.
PSALM 16:11 NIV

Liz Gliem was raised in a Christian family on a farm. When her mother lost a two-year battle against cancer, her family fell into a dark time. Throughout her teen years, Liz felt angry with God and kept Him at a distance. Her parents had loved the Lord with all their hearts, and what they suffered didn't seem fair. When Liz was in college, her dad had a redemptive encounter with Jesus. No longer bent by grief, he came to life again, and seeing her dad transformed drew Liz back to faith too. When Liz heard about Iris and contemplated a farming ministry in Africa, her dad was her biggest supporter. He was behind her 100 percent.

Our 126-acre farm in Mozambique beckoned Liz, and we were thrilled when she decided to relocate. Her dad and sister traveled with Liz to help her settle into her new home before returning to the States. One Sunday, after church, Liz found her dad dead on the beach. No one knew why or how it had happened. She was utterly blindsided. She and her sister buried their father in Mozambique and then flew back to the States. Her world flipped upside down. She felt confused, bitter, and angry, and she had no intention of returning to Mozambique. Her greatest fear was that her grief would once again send her running away from God.

Thankfully, Liz was able to find God's special nearness and His peace in the midst of her tragedy. Jesus encountered her too. It was just a whisper—a simple knowing in the depth of her bones that she would return to Mozambique. She knew it would not always be easy, but she obeyed Him nonetheless. Years later, this woman of God is making an incredible impact through farming, discipleship, and disaster response.

Tragedies happen, and when they bring your life to a halt, choose to worship. You are not entitled to a problem-free life, but God will speak to you in times of grief and mourning. And if you choose to draw near to Him during times of pain, you have an opportunity to build and fortify the foundations of your faith. His presence will surpass your emotions until you know that He is good, no matter what. We are also not entitled to know all the answers. They wouldn't bring us peace anyway; only Jesus can do that. His promise is that no matter what happens, He will be with us. That doesn't mean it won't be difficult, but do your best to avoid getting stuck in self-pity. Keep your eyes fixed on Jesus. He's your King, your Creator, your Redeemer, and your Defender. Because of His sacrifice, death has lost its sting. We have an eternal home. Truly, He turns our mourning into joy.

Lord, I trust You in the outcome that I can't predict right now. I trust You in the things I don't know. You know our hours, our seasons, and our times. Everything is in the palm of Your hand.

- Listen quietly: "For the Holy Spirit makes God's fatherhood real to us as he whispers into our innermost being, 'You are God's beloved child!'" (Romans 8:16).

- Examine your heart. Pray the last verses of Psalm 139, asking Him to search your heart and test your anxious thoughts (See Psalm 139).

- Continue to be obedient while you are grieving: "The Holy Spirit has set you apart to be God's holy ones, obedient followers of Jesus Christ" (1 Peter 1:2).

Liz on the Iris farm

Christ, the Rock

Everyone who hears my teaching and applies it to his life can be compared to a wise man who built his house on an unshakable foundation.

<small>MATTHEW 7:24</small>

Mel and Joyce Tari lead World Mission, an international ministry that partners with churches and ministries worldwide to bring the gospel to all nations. Rolland and I have been close friends with them for decades, and Mel was the best man in our wedding. He grew up in Indonesia and has witnessed miracles around the globe. God graciously provided for their family home, which they had lived in for twenty-five years while raising three sons, but at one point, their financial situation became challenging. They struggled to pay bills, and the bank threatened to foreclose on their mortgage multiple times. They sought legal help, but after paying high fees for a year, they made zero progress. The upkeep and monthly payments exceeded their budget. Expenses mounted. Pipes burst. They joked that the house "improved" after every flood, and the last plumbing disaster felt like a sign. The workmen even boxed up the family's belongings and placed them in the garage.

The Taris worried about where they would go. They knew that friends would let them stay in guest rooms if it came to that, but that obviously wasn't ideal. Their credit would be ruined if they couldn't sell the house. Despite the many "what ifs," they focused on God through the battle of the mind. Joyce felt overwhelmed but prayed for a good attitude. She gave thanks for the twenty-five years they enjoyed in their home. They wouldn't be able to keep all their belongings, but they would treasure each wonderful memory.

Then a friend in real estate came up with a creative solution. They negotiated a deal with investors who saw the potential in the damaged house, and the investors bought the Taris' home at full price! Everyone won. Mel and Joyce paid off their mortgage and even made a small profit, but searching for a condo within their new budget was depressing. Joyce found a property online that she was excited about, but it seemed too pricey. She crossed it off her list of potential places and committed herself to gratitude regardless of where they ended up. Low and behold, their realtor later took them to that same condo. It was small but nicely renovated. Walking inside, they felt joy and peace at once. Their realtor found a way to make the purchase within their budget, and for Joyce, getting the home she had written off felt like an unexpected gift from God.

Had Mel and Joyce focused solely on the number in their bank account, they would have lost a tremendous amount of sleep throughout the entire process. Instead, when things seemed impossible, they remembered that God has always been their provider. They kept an eternal perspective. They wanted to bring people to Jesus rather than worry about this life or earthly possessions. They left behind the pressures of keeping up a large house and have greater freedom to visit their grandchildren and minister around the world. They see blessings in downsizing. God taught them not to hang on to yesterday's blessings but to hold all things loosely. Situations change, but we stand firm on the One who never changes.

God, thank You that You will finish what You've started in my life. You are bringing me into my future and my destiny in You. In the journey I am on, help me build my life upon the Rock.

- "Constantly chase after the realm of God's kingdom and the righteousness that proceeds from him. Then all these less important things will be given to you abundantly" (Matthew 6:33).

- Keep the right perspective on earthly possessions: "You can't worship the true God while enslaved to the god of money!" (Matthew 6:24).

- Trust God completely: "With all your heart rely on him to guide you, and he will lead you in every decision you make" (Proverbs 3:5).

Rolland, Heidi, Joyce, and Mel

Ground Zero

Our struggle is not against flesh and blood, but against the rulers, against the authorities, against the powers of this dark world and against the spiritual forces of evil in the heavenly realms.

EPHESIANS 6:11 NIV

One day, while driving to our university property, I looked out my window and did not see our Iris Maringanha church along the way as usual. I thought that was strange. I figured I had somehow looked in the wrong spot and continued to our Iris University meeting. On the way home, I looked again and found that the church had literally disappeared. There was no indication it had ever been there. I got out of the truck and saw that not only had our church been totally destroyed but the ground was also completely cleared! There was no rubble, and the land had been raked clean.

I remembered Ephesians 6 and prayed about putting on the armor of God. It was nighttime, but as I prayed, I strongly felt we needed to rebuild the church right away. I asked our student pastors if they wanted to help, and a large group joined me almost at once. God gave us supernatural hope to start again without pause. We brought headlights, hoes, and shovels. I was so encouraged to rebuild together with my brothers. It felt imperative that we start digging the new foundation the very same day. If we left the church destroyed, then the Christian witness in that village might have been completely wiped out. Follow the Holy Spirit's timing! Don't be afraid to wait if that's what you sense, but if He gives you an urgent call to do something, obey immediately.

It was challenging to start from ground zero. We feared that hostile people might destroy the new building too. Remember that God has called us to live in peace with people of other faiths. Our battle is not against flesh and blood but takes place in the spiritual realm. So we put on our spiritual armor and dug, dug, dug. We ended up rebuilding a much better church, a Shalom soccer field, and water wells. The church currently serves as a base of operations for feeding spiritual and physical food to thousands of internally displaced people living in Maringanha village. Through our outreach, we are strengthening relationships with the chief and community leaders. We now work together in unity to meet the needs of the people of Maringanha. The chief asked us to put electricity in our church so that the people could worship at night. After more than eighteen years of outreach, they gave us a piece of property to build a sanitation block for the internally displaced people. The new church and wells have become a central gathering place, and many people are meeting Jesus. God completely turned things around.

In life it can sometimes feel like whatever we've built has been leveled to the ground. Whatever the battle, put on the armor of God and pray in the Spirit on all occasions. If someone you love feels leveled to the ground, embrace them. Ask the Holy Spirit to give you words of comfort. We win spiritual battles together, and God gives courage and hope for every circumstance.

God, I put on Your armor to fight every spiritual battle. Your wrap-around shield protects me from every fiery dart. I stand alert, ready to share the good news.

- Read Ephesians 6:10-20 out loud. Put on your spiritual armor for every battle. Pray passionately about each situation you face and "rise victorious" (Ephesians 6:13).

- Speak God's Word, your sword, over your thoughts: "Embrace the power of salvation's full deliverance, like a helmet to protect your thoughts from lies" (Ephesians 6:17-18).

- When God shows you what to do, obey immediately. Even if it feels like starting from ground zero, join with others and rebuild together.

Maringanha Church (2020)

Time to Bloom

*Abraham, when called to go to a place he would later
receive as his inheritance, obeyed and went, even though
he did not know where he was going.*
Hebrews 11:8 NIV

Laura Taranto was my faithful, beloved assistant for
five years. In 2017, we traveled to Europe, and she was
deeply touched by how many refugees received Jesus. She
sensed that God was pleased with her eight-year season
with us in Pemba and that he was inviting her to something new. Laura was inspired by other Iris leaders who
followed Jesus to pioneer ministries globally, and she felt
called back to Europe in particular. She knew God had a
beautiful story for her life but didn't know what it would
look like. The next summer, when it was time to transition, she felt mixed emotions. The world had dramati-
cally changed, including escalating terrorism and restric-
tive visa policies, which greatly reduced our international

team. Though heartbroken to leave the team, Laura knew God was leading her. She gave Him her yes!

A friend discovered that Laura could apply for Italian citizenship through Laura's great-grandfather. It felt like a total miracle. Laura's dad was thrilled and helped throughout the entire process. He even bought the family an Italian flag. When they applied, they found out that the process could take two years. Laura was disheartened. Shortly after, Laura faced a serious medical problem and needed surgery, leaving her even more discouraged. She went to Europe anyway and lived with friends in Holland while she recovered. Then our Iris Germany team helped her move to Berlin and acquire a language learning visa. God gave her an apartment in one day! She knew God was with her, but it was extremely challenging. When Cyclone Kenneth hit Mozambique, Laura wished she could help with the disaster response. Instead, she was taking beginning German classes and still recovering. This wasn't how she pictured her new season. She deeply missed helping those in need and felt like she'd been demoted.

Nevertheless, Laura continued to seek God and remembered Zechariah 4:10 about not despising small beginnings. She connected with Shapoor (whom I mentioned earlier in this book) and went on a ministry trip to Turkey. She found a welcoming church community and hosted a delicious, traditional Thanksgiving with new friends. This was a change since she'd spent the last eight Thanksgivings in Mozambique, usually on outreach. The very next day, her dad shared incredible news: both Laura and her dad were officially Italian citizens! Laura was absolutely amazed at God's timing. I called her from the Israeli desert to celebrate with her. After such a challenging journey, this felt like clear confirmation of God's call. Laura went on another trip to Turkey and Greece, and ministering in a refugee camp was a dream come true.

God's plans unfolded one step at a time. He gave Laura a vision to start Witness, an organization that ministers to refugees and shares their stories. This organization tied together Laura's passions, talents, and experiences in a splendid way. Pay attention to your talents and whatever makes your heart come alive because God uses everything. He is weaving together a beautiful story in your life. Like a seed planted in the ground, it will take time to grow, but when you see the fruit that God produces, you will be amazed.

God, thank You for Your faithfulness in my
last season. Your plans for my life are good.
Lead me wherever You want and give me Your
vision for my life. I give You my yes.

- Give yourself permission to rest during transitions. Don't worry about having all the answers or seeing the full picture. Take one step at a time.

- Remember His faithfulness: "All the ways of the Lord are loving and faithful for those who follow the ways of his covenant" (Psalm 25:10).

- Trust: "It is the Lord who directs your life, for each step you take is ordained by God to bring you closer to your destiny" (Proverbs 20:24).

Laura visiting a refugee family in their tent in Lesvos, Greece

No More Sorrow

Death, tell me, where is your victory?
Tell me death, where is your sting?
1 Corinthians 15:55

In August 2018, we had an Iris family gathering with our teams from around the world. We met to share stories of what God was doing in the nations and to encourage one other. During the meeting, our friends, Brian and Pamela Jourden, received a terrifying phone call. Their 23-year-old son, Bryson, suffered a tragic accident while rock climbing with ministry school friends in South Africa. He had fallen and was in a coma. At once we all began to pray and cry out for Bryson's healing. Brian boarded a plane immediately. During his flight connection, he received the call that Bryson had died. Pamela had stayed with us and was in my arms, releasing Bryson into the arms of Jesus at the very moment she received word that he had passed. In their grief, the Jourdens took solace knowing that their son was in heaven. They knew he would want to stay in heaven when he saw the Father's face. Every good dream is met in the Father.

As the Jourdens grieved, they imagined a river with two banks. One bank represented the importance of not asking why because we cannot always know the answer. The other bank represented not blaming anyone. The Jourdens committed themselves to staying within those banks, not asking why this tragedy had happened and not blaming themselves or God or Bryson's friends at the cliff. When people did not give them the kind of support for which they had hoped, they still chose not to blame but to be grateful for those who *did* surround them with love and prayer. Some days they stayed in the shallows of that metaphorical river. Other days they sank deep into sorrow. They made efforts to laugh and feel light-hearted again so that grief would not ferment into bitterness. They made the goodness of God their bedrock and worshiped. They stayed mindful of the good in their lives. They didn't understand, but they knew God would not leave them broken forever and that something beautiful would grow from these ashes. New things would be birthed in their lives and in their family.

I had a powerful impression of Bryson riding a horse in heaven. He was completely whole. Although we pray for healing, no matter what happens, our ultimate prize is living eternally face-to-face with God. Death has lost its sting. This world is not our eternal home. The realm of heaven is real; it's not a fairy tale. If someone isn't healed on earth, there is a place without sorrow and suffering that the Bible tells us about. God is our Healer and holds us safely in His hand, and absolutely nothing can take us away from Him.

God, thank You that You will wipe every tear and eliminate death. In heaven, "no one will mourn or weep any longer. The pain of wounds will no longer exist."[3]

3   Revelation 21:4

- Remember that God promises beauty for ashes. When all seems lost, remember that one day something new will grow or be birthed in your life.

- Pass *through* the valley of weeping with God: "You are the revelation-light in my darkness, and in your brightness I can see the path ahead" (Psalm 18:28).

- Have an eternal perspective: "Lord, you have always been our eternal home, our hiding place from generation to generation" (Psalm 90:1).

The Jourdens' last photo with Bryson (on the far right)

God of the Impossible

Ask and it will be given to you; seek and you will find;
knock and the door will be opened to you. For everyone
who asks receives; the one who seeks finds; and to the one
who knocks, the door will be opened.

MATTHEW 7:7–8 NIV

Jamal Awale is a twenty-five-year-old who walks
in great love and wisdom. After Jamal's parents passed
away, he and his three siblings moved into our Iris Village
of Joy. Losing parents while you are young is devastating and one of the most difficult challenges in life. Jamal
didn't know what would happen to him, but as he learned
about God as his Father, he found his forever family.

Last year, Jamal went through another immense challenge: his home was destroyed by Cyclone Kenneth. Made
only of mud and bamboo, it was completely flooded and
collapsed. At first, he didn't tell anyone what happened as
he suffered his own storm of negative emotions. It became

a struggle for him to pray. He questioned why God would let this happen to him after he had already gone through so much. He felt hopeless, frustrated, and angry at God. He didn't have enough to rent even a temporary home. Everything was washed away. Then he remembered lessons he learned already. He stood on the truth that God is God of the impossible. He determined not to let the troubles he was going through cause him to doubt God or question his goodness.

Jamal decided to reach out and help others. He joined the Iris Relief team to rebuild other people's homes. As he served neighbors who had lost everything, almost no one knew of his situation. Then his friend Pascoal, a leader on our Iris media team, came to visit. He asked if he could make a video about what had happened. Jamal didn't know if the video would help, but he figured it couldn't hurt. As it happened, many more people watched the video than Jamal expected. They sent aid, and we were quickly able to build Jamal a much better block home and furnish it. God never forgets His children. We were blessed to be the family Jamal needed.

Jamal learned many things during his experience. First, trust God and learn to wait on Him. His answer does not always come right away. Do not give up—no matter what it costs or how long it takes. Be confident and keep moving forward on your path with God. He sees you, and at the right time, He will respond. He knows what you need and what would bless your life. The Bible says to ask, seek, and knock. It doesn't say to sit still and do nothing. Don't tell yourself that you are too poor or not good enough, believing that you will never receive your blessing. Do whatever you *can* do in your situation. Put your hope in God; He always has a solution no matter the circumstances. Keep hoping and working. Don't forget what you already know: He is God of the impossible!

God, You are God of the impossible. Your Word says everyone who asks receives. You are the One who opens doors. I am asking, seeking, and knocking. Give me courage and confidence as I wait on You. Make me a faithful friend who trusts in Your goodness and never gives up.

- Wait patiently even if it feels like a long time: "I waited and waited and waited some more, patiently, knowing God would come through for me" (Psalm 40:1).

- Have faith. Trust in God and be confident in His Word. Never give up: "At last, he bent down and listened to my cry" (Psalm 40:1).

- It is powerful to go through challenges and overcome: "Be brave and courageous, and never lose hope" (Psalm 27:14). Courage gives us hope for victory!

Jamal and Heidi

God of Miracles

Eli answered her, "Go in peace. And may the God of Israel give you what you have asked of him."
"Think well of me—and pray for me!" she said, and went her way. Then she ate heartily, her face radiant.
1 SAMUEL 1:17–18 MSG

Fabiana Liu dreamed of becoming a mother. When she and her husband, Isaac, were ready for children, they learned it might take them a year to get pregnant. That first year came and went, and to Fabiana, it felt like life was on pause while she and Isaac continued to try. The doctor reassured them they were too young to worry, but Fabiana struggled to enjoy life. Their friends were having babies. And then those same friends had second and third babies. The wait was painful, and Fabiana feared she would never have children. What would she tell people on Christmas and Mother's Day? She had to fight the lies in her head that told her she wasn't worthy or that God might not think of her as a good mom.

Fabiana asked the Holy Spirit to show her God's truth, and the story of Hannah gave her hope. She didn't want to turn bitter; she wanted to keep believing that her dream would come true. Her best friend and sister-in-law both got pregnant again, while Fabiana got more negative pregnancy test results. Despite herself, she grew frustrated and sad. One week, Fabiana was exploring options for adoption when a prophet whom she didn't know visited her church. He told her, "God sees the adoption papers, but He says you are not adopting now. He is giving you a child. You are going to travel the world with your child and tell the story." Fabiana treasured the prophet's words and made a conscious decision to keep on living while she waited. She and Isaac planted a church and ministered around the world. She intentionally celebrated others. She hosted baby showers with a smile, keeping her tears for her private moments. She rejoiced when others received what she wanted most. It was hard, but she discovered she was stronger than she thought. And the waiting gave her profound compassion for others who also waited for a miracle.

Isaac and Fabiana decided to visit a fertility doctor and start treatment after four years of trying. They shared their struggle in their community, and the shame they felt disappeared when they met other couples going through similar struggles. They wished they had sought support sooner. Then after her second fertility treatment, Fabiana suffered a terrible car accident. She made sure to tell the medics that she might be pregnant so that they would only use local anesthetic to stitch her injuries as opposed to more powerful medications that may harm her baby. During fertility treatment, she took two pregnancy tests. Both were negative, and again she was devastated.

Fabiana surrendered her dream, praying to find satisfaction in God alone. What she didn't know was that the test results were wrong; she really *was* pregnant! Her pregnancy proved to be incredibly challenging, and Fabiana fought to believe that her baby would be healthy despite the strong medications she had been given after her car accident. But beautiful Elisa was born perfect and healthy. Now Isaac and Fabiana are some of the most joyful parents I know. They endure sleepless nights like all new parents, but they don't complain about them. They know how long they waited and how hard they fought for their promise. They are forever grateful to the God of miracles, who taught them that waiting time is not wasted time.

God, You are still the God of miracles. Fill my heart with hope as I wait for my promises. You are not too late. You are always on time. You still do impossible things, and You have the last word.

- Write down any lies that you believe and invite the Holy Spirit to show you the truth. Declare God's truth from Bible verses and speak prophetic words over yourself.

- Celebrate others even as you pray and wait for your promise: "When you succeed, we will celebrate and shout for joy" (Psalm 20:5).

- Don't put life on hold because of what you don't have. Keep living: "Gaze upon him, join your life with his, and joy will come" (Psalm 34:5).

Isaac, Fabiana, and Elisa

Unto Me

Mary said, "Behold the maidservant of the Lord!
Let it be to me according to your word."
And the angel departed from her.
LUKE 1:38 NKJV

My amazing, encouraging father used to tell me I would one day attend Stanford University like he did. We later found out that I had severe dyslexia and could barely read, so I was put in remedial classes. Teachers told me I would never attend university, and my classmates mocked and tormented me. I felt incredibly stupid. Stanford was certainly out of the question, which must have been a great disappointment for my dad, even though he was never unkind about it. After I came to faith at age sixteen, God miraculously rewired my brain, and I could suddenly read with ease! Pushing past low expectations, I was accepted to and graduated from a private Christian university.

Another part of my father's story was that he became an atheist while at Stanford. No one could answer his questions about God to his satisfaction. I dreamed that someday I might share the true love of God at this university, and when I *did* receive an opportunity to speak at Stanford years later, I was overwhelmed with the conviction that God can do anything with anyone. Then the Iris board asked me if I wanted to attend a professional training course for CEOs of nonprofit organizations at none other than Stanford. As intimidated as I was when I applied, I also knew that nothing is impossible with God. When Laura, my assistant, handed my acceptance letter to me, I broke into tears. It felt like an astounding miracle that I would have the opportunity to study at my father's alma mater.

Having been taunted and bullied in school affected me. Even after getting a PhD, I still felt stupid. If anyone commented on my intelligence, I felt miserable and questioned myself. I battled fears that I would be mocked at a prestigious university like Stanford. What if I had to spell something without the help of spell check while I was in front of the other CEOs? Despite my fears, I understood that God led me there, and He would help me shine for Him. Prayer counselors also helped me pray about the ways I had been mocked and belittled. The Lord spoke to my heart that He had given me a keen mind. I sobbed like a baby and finally stopped believing the lie.

Once I overcame the lie that I was stupid, I developed a strong desire to help others, particularly poverty-stricken Northern Mozambicans, who believed they could never go to university. What if the Lord could open the door for them to study at Stanford? To make a long story short, four of our students earned scholarships to attend a summer study program at Stanford. Two of those students were among my very first elementary school class, which I had started under a baobab tree after the Lord called me to build a university. Sending them to Stanford was an astounding experience for all of us. Academics may have led my father away from faith, but our Mozambican students boldly shared their faith at that same university. Later in life, I led my father to faith. Another miracle. The whole story feels like one impossible dream coming to pass after another. It was and is beyond anything I could have hoped or imagined.

God, nothing is impossible for You. All Your promises are yes and amen. They are not yes and no. Help me believe and walk in everything You've said about me. Be it done unto me as You have said.

- Don't strive; trust God with your promises: "Yahweh is the one who makes a way in the sea, a pathway in the mighty waters" (Isaiah 43:16).

- Worship God and keep going: "Don't yield to fear. All you need to do is to keep on believing" (Mark 5:36).

- Multiply your victory by helping others secure their victory: "Thank God for giving us the victory as conquerors through our Lord Jesus, the Anointed One" (1 Corinthians 15:57).

Heidi and the students who attended the Stanford summer study program at Iris University campus

Submit to God

Trust in the LORD with all your heart
and lean not on your own understanding;
in all your ways submit to him,
and he will make your paths straight.

PROVERBS 3:5–6 NIV

Esther Scheele is one of the sweetest, most servant-hearted women of God I know. She was on our team in Mozambique for nearly three years, and to work in Africa was her dream come true. Our team went through several frustrating periods of time when conflicts with radical insurgents in northern Mozambique spurred changes in visa policies for foreigners. Esther was among those who lost permission to stay within the country and was forced to leave within ninety days. She believed she would return, but despite many attempts, we couldn't obtain a new visa for her. She never got to say goodbye or have closure. In fact, other team members had to pack all her belongings and ship them to the States.

Esther loved Mozambique and had felt genuinely called to it. She was passionate about serving the needy, and she cultivated deep friendships while there. It was not her plan to leave, nor did she sense God asking her to transition. She expected to stay in Mozambique for at least ten years, and it was as if a door had suddenly and unexpectedly shut. Heartbroken, Esther couldn't understand why her dream had been cut short. She worried she wasn't good enough, or maybe God was punishing her, or perhaps she simply lacked what it took to live out the calling on her heart. Esther chose to turn to God in prayer and bring all her questions and insecurities directly to Him. She prayed heartfelt psalms like 73 and 31. She was honest with God about her pain but continued to declare God's promises and His Word. She let Him reassure her, beyond her fears and doubts, that He would accomplish His purposes. She learned to embrace pain, die to herself, and trust that God was doing something for His greater glory. God showed Esther that her value, identity, and purpose are not found in what she does or where she serves but in relationship with Him. He would care for the people of Mozambique if she could not.

God is the one who provides, encourages, redeems, and saves. He is faithful to complete the good work He starts in each of us. He will bless, protect, and provide for us, and He is better than we can imagine. We are not entitled to have all the answers to our questions on this side of eternity. We lean on Him when we don't understand. We let Him use every disappointment to draw us into greater intimacy, greater prayer, and greater revelation. Esther now works for an organization called Watts of Love, which brings solar lights to poor communities around the world. Through Esther, Watts of Love was able to send solar lights to us in Mozambique, and they are a tremendous resource for internally displaced people. Beyond her disappointment, God strengthened and affirmed her. He gave her even greater vision for His plans and her dreams. His ways are always greater than ours.

Lord, when everything seems confusing, even the opposite of what I want, I still choose to lavish my love on You. I trust You with all my heart and lean on You. I submit to You. You will make my path straight.

- Pray the psalms and express your emotions to God: "I'm desperate, Lord! I throw myself upon you, for you alone are my God!" (Psalm 31:14).

- Surrender: "Every morning I lay out the pieces of my life on the altar and wait for your fire to fall upon my heart" (Psalm 5:3).

- Do your part. Be faithful in whatever you can do to follow Him, then be open for the unexpected. Humbly submit to His leadership.

Esther in Mozambique

Light of the World

Blessed are the poor in spirit,
for theirs is the kingdom of heaven.
MATTHEW 5:3 NIV

In October of 2017, radical insurgents started attacking villages in Cabo Delgado, where our home in northern Mozambique has been since 2003. We heard reports of villages burned to ash and people brutally killed by beheading. Many fled south fearing for their lives. Then in April 2019, Cyclone Kenneth hit northern Mozambique, destroying thousands of homes.

By 2020, terrorism escalated to war. Radical insurgents increased the intensity of their attacks in Cabo Delgado Province, and the atmosphere remains extremely tense. We talk among our discipleship groups about being prepared to die for the gospel and counting it all joy to give our lives for the One who is worthy. It continues to be one of the most difficult seasons we have ever known, but the Lord has brought us to deeper places of trust and devotion.

These days we frequently sit with people as tears of sorrow stream down their faces. They have scars on their bodies and on their hearts. We hold them in our arms and comfort them with prayer as they share story after story of dreadful tragedy. Countless people's homes were burned to the ground as they fled in terror with only the clothes on their backs. Multitudes slept in the bush for days without food or water. Many have lost family members. Some have witnessed gruesome murders. According to statistics from the United Nations, over two hundred fifty thousand people are internally displaced in Pemba and the surrounding area.[4] Not only are these people desperately hungry, but they're also emotionally traumatized.

We remain full of prayer, hope, song, and dance as we seek to love people toward healing and freedom: "Blessed are the peacemakers, for they will be called children of God. Blessed are those who are persecuted because of righteousness, for theirs is the kingdom of heaven" (Matthew 5:9-10 NIV). We are the salt of the earth and the light of the world. We are the feet on the ground, and we distribute food aid and solar audio Bibles to nearly twenty thousand people a day. Wherever we brought spiritual and physical food to villages ravaged by the cyclone, we found extreme hunger and an openness

---

[4]   "Cabo Delgado," UNHCR, August 2020, https://reporting.unhcr.org.

for God's love. Many accepted Jesus as their Savior for the first time. As we witness the resilience of our Mozambican brothers and sisters, our own faith is strengthened. Hope swells in our hearts because we see God moving in the midst of horrific storms. He is in control. We never could have imagined how God would turn these devastating tragedies around, but He is opening hearts to the gospel of peace.

God, take me deep into Your presence where I am no longer afraid. My life does not belong to me. It completely belongs to You. Take me further and deeper than ever before, into a place of compassion, to a place of greater courage. Jesus, You are worthy of it all.

- Shine brightly: "Your lives light up the world. Let others see your light from a distance" (Matthew 5:14).

- Do good works: "It is always beautiful and profitable for believers to do good works" (Titus 3:8).

- Go deeper still: "The Lord alone is our radiant hope and we trust in him with all our hearts. His wrap-around presence will strengthen us" (Psalm 33:20).

Ministering after Cyclone Kenneth

No Matter What

If we are thrown into the blazing furnace,
the God we serve is able to deliver us from it...
but even if he does not, we want you to know,
Your Majesty, that we will not serve your gods.
DANIEL 3:17–18 NIV

When Cyclone Kenneth devastated northern Mozambique in April of 2019, it wiped out homes and harvest fields, leaving entire villages and islands without food or shelter. The people ate whatever they could find, including unripe coconuts that caused serious diarrhea and even death among children. James and Jessica Brewer, members of our Iris media team in Pemba, recorded video footage whenever we brought food, supplies, and God's love to villages. Several months after the cyclone, James and Jessica's baby daughter, Grace, fell sick with seizures and a high fever. The clinic tested for all common tropical diseases but could not reach a diagnosis. Grace's health continued to decline, and James and Jessica wished they could suffer the pain on her behalf. It is heart-wrenching for parents to watch their child suffer.

As Grace fought for her life, James and Jessica evaluated their faith like never before. They related to Shadrach, Meshach, and Abednego, who committed to serve God even when they were thrown into a furnace. James and Jessica retained their hope by meditating on God's promises of abundant life. They held every thought captive in prayer and anchored their hearts in the reality of God's nature. Their Iris family surrounded them with prayer and testimonies of God's faithfulness too. James and Jessica understood from experience that He is a God of miracles and a good Father who loved Grace even more than they did. They truly believed He would heal Grace; however, they also prepared themselves for their worst fear if He did not heal her. Together, James and Jessica decided that their yes to God would remain. They would never quit. Instead, they would love and trust Him and continue to serve the poor in Mozambique. And if Grace died, then they knew that she would be in heaven with God.

Grace's health situation became so urgent that the Brewers' insurance company paid to have Grace, James, and Jessica medically evacuated to South Africa. As they prepared to depart from the airport, I was returning from a ministry trip. My husband was at the airport to pick me up, and he prayed with James and Jess, telling them that Grace's symptoms reminded him of the time I had bilharzia, a disease caused by parasitic flatworms. And when I arrived, I told them I felt the Lord showing me that Grace's illness was indeed a result of bilharzia. It felt like God was getting their attention.

When the Brewers reached South Africa, doctors performed extensive tests on Grace and found no discernible cause for her illness. So Jessica specifically asked for the test for bilharzia, and sure enough, that was Grace's ailment. The parasite was found just in time before it had reached Grace's kidneys. It was a miracle. James and Jessica's experience left them with a radical empathy for parents in Mozambique who did everything they could but still sometimes lost children to disease or starvation. They returned with greater focus, vision, and determination to help people who lacked resources. Trials cultivate our character and our hearts. They strengthen our perseverance, mature our faith, and give us greater hope, just as the book of James teaches.

God, give us courage to not bow our knee to fear. You are God who parted the Red Sea, and You can conquer the impossible. Bring light and hope to situations that seem desolate, broken, or impossible.

- Run to God, your refuge: "God, you're such a safe and powerful place to find refuge! You're a proven help in time of trouble" (Psalm 46:1).

- Worship until you find rest and peace. Worship and pray alone and with others who will bring you strength.

- Remain in hope: "Quiet your heart in his presence and pray; keep hope alive as you long for God to come through for you" (Psalm 37:7).

James, Jess, and Grace in Mozambique

DAY 37

Wait under His Wings

But those who wait on the LORD
Shall renew their strength;
They shall mount up with wings like eagles,
They shall run and not be weary,
They shall walk and not faint.

ISAIAH 40:31 NKJV

Whenever we distribute food, we always share the gospel. We listen to people's stories and offer to pray with them. During a recent outreach, I met a family in the middle of an extraordinary crisis. Radical insurgents had attacked their village, and Diamon and Vitoria fled into the bush in terror. Vitoria had been holding her newborn baby in her arms, and Diamon grabbed their toddler. But they had lost sight of their four other children—ages eight, ten, fourteen, and sixteen—among the chaos. They later found that their home had been burned to the ground, so the clothes on their backs were all that they had.

Diamon, Vitoria, Vitoria's sister, and their youngest children spent four nights sleeping in the bush. They had no food and tried everything to find their four missing children, but they eventually had to sell their cell phone to pay for a ride to Pemba. When I met them, they had not heard any recent news from home. They borrowed phones to make calls, but no one answered. As I listened to them, I thought of my own grandchildren. What if I lost them? My heart broke for these parents. Vitoria and I held each other, weeping and praying for a miracle in the name of Jesus. Our team bought them a new phone to keep calling around in search of their children.

Whenever we are in the middle of a trial, we experience a waiting period of uncertainty, not knowing how the trial will end. Whether that waiting period lasts a day, a week, a month, or even several years, we know that God is always good. Psalm 91 is one of my favorite prayers for painful waiting seasons. When we find ourselves roaming around in the unknown, we can hide ourselves in God, our refuge. We can trust Him no matter what. Isaiah 40:31 is another powerful waiting prayer. He renews our strength as we wait and mounts us up with wings like eagles, which soar at great heights to gain an even higher vantage point. They catch the wind.

Today, all of Diamon and Vitoria's children are safe. For this we give God glory, honor, and praise. After we purchased them a cell phone, they called and called and called every person they could. At last, their children were found hiding in the bush and brought to a nearby village. We wholeheartedly rejoice with them over this miracle. If you are in a time of waiting, keep praying. Let God carry you when you feel too weak to run or even walk. Let Him shield you as you hide under His wings.

Teach me how to wait on You, Lord. Thank You for hiding me under Your wings and shielding me. As I wait on You, You will restore my strength. I will mount up on wings like an eagle. I will run and not grow weary, walk and not faint.

- Hide in God: "Protect me from harm...hide me within the shelter of your embrace, under your outstretched wings" (Psalm 17:8).

- Wait on God. Our timing is not always God's timing: "I will watch and wait for you, O God, throughout the night" (Psalm 130:6).

- Be like an eagle. Let the Holy Spirit lift you higher. Ask God for His perspective and for the wind of His Spirit to carry you.

Heidi meeting Diamon and Vitoria

Engage the Process

*We know that in all things God works
for the good of those who love him,
who have been called according to his purpose.*
ROMANS 8:28 NIV

Tony and Pamela Maxwell, the administrative direc-
tors of Iris Harvest School, sat on their porch in the
United States to enjoy a morning devotional after a busy
holiday season. They had been living in community in
Mozambique, so it was nice to have the house to themselves. Once they were ready to return inside, they were
alarmed to find that the door was locked. They were
trapped on a porch elevated ten feet up from the ground.
Tony tried to climb down a pillar, but the railing gave
way. He fell to the ground and suffered a vertebral com-
pression fracture, four pelvic fractures, and a displaced
sacral fracture that required bone screws. He endured
severe pain for a month and discomfort for many more.

Tony did not ask, "Why did this happen?" Instead, he asked, "What does God want to teach me through this?" He believed God's plan for his life was perfect even if he could not understand why God had allowed the accident.

Tony's physical recovery was long and painful. When he couldn't sleep, he listened to worship music, particularly old hymns. The following song lyric touched him deeply: "When dark trials come and my heart is filled with the weight of doubt, I will praise Him still."[5] One night, Tony played the song on repeat, and the presence of God filled the room as he had never experienced before. Weeping, he committed to praising God through every trial; God knew best. And each morning, as Tony's brother and wife swung his legs around and helped him out of bed, billions of nerves he never knew existed brought tears to his eyes, and his physical therapy was no less agonizing. However painful it was, he knew this was the only way forward. His other choice was to remain bedridden for the rest of his life. Either he would get up, or he wouldn't. He used the motto "no pain, no gain" and embraced the process daily.

Dwelling on questions of *why* does not help us overcome. We can choose to be angry, stomp our feet, and complain, but we eventually return to God's sovereignty, love, compassion, and mercy. If we can trust Him with eternal salvation, then we can trust Him to get us through

---

[5]   Fernando Ortega, "I Will Praise Him, Still," track 8 on *This Bright Hour*, Myrrh Records, 1997.

trials. He is more than enough. We want to speak God's Word and truth over our thoughts and "run the rats out of the room" by taking captive the worries and fears that run rampant. This is true for physical and emotional pains too. We must engage with God's process for our healing. For example, Tony's greatest fear was having a permanent disability, so he did everything he could to achieve victory and trusted God with the rest. He realized that when God is all you have, God is all you need. Tony's now able to run for miles and nearly pain free. God is faithful!

God, You work all things for my good, even things that feel challenging. Help me take every thought captive and believe Your truth. Give me hope and courage today. Through trials and whatever I face, I will praise You still.

- Do not ask why God allowed something to happen or adopt a victim mentality.

- Do ask what He wants to teach you through your circumstances.

- Keep praising: "Even during this crisis in my soul I will be radiant with joy, filled with praise for your love and mercy" (Psalm 31:7).

Rolland, Heidi, Pamela, and Tony

You Are on Assignment

Be saturated in prayer throughout each day...
Tell him every detail of your life, then God's
wonderful peace that transcends human understanding,
will make the answers known to you through Jesus Christ.
PHILIPPIANS 4:6-7

Wherever God takes you, you are on assignment. I learned this during an extraordinarily challenging journey to Mozambique during COVID-19 border closures. I was with my sister in California after ministering in Asia when I felt a strong impression from God that I needed to get home to Mozambique—immediately. My assistant booked a flight through Ethiopia, and I started to pack. Normally that task takes me a while, but this time I literally threw clothes into my suitcase and ordered an Uber to LAX. I was in such a rush that I forgot my passport and wallet, but my sister was able to drive them to me just in time.

When I reached Washington, DC, most flights were already canceled. As I waited, I spent hours in prayer while walking around the airport. I felt I was on assignment to pray for the United States. The delay was so long that I missed my connecting flight, and the airline couldn't guarantee that I'd make it to Ethiopia, but I felt I needed to keep going. I *did* manage to make it to the Ethiopian airport, where hundreds of people were jammed into a small space. Some wore masks, and some did not. Some coughed while others screamed. People were even hitting each other. Everyone was urgently trying to reach their destination before borders closed.

Again, I felt the impression that I was on assignment. I met with aid workers, people from other faiths, and believers. I talked and prayed with individuals whom the Lord highlighted to me. I didn't push through the crowds; I waited. Then the airline put me in a hotel while I waited for a flight, and after three days, I boarded the very last plane to Mozambique. It was undoubtedly a miracle, but when we landed, only people with Mozambican passports were permitted to enter the country. My permanent residence is in Mozambique, and I truly feel Mozambican, but the customs officer told me that foreigners were not allowed into the country. I was crushed. I struggled to stay hopeful but remembered every promise of God, and I took courage in seeing how far He'd brought me already.

I sensed God telling me to stand my ground. The airline miraculously held the plane for me while I pleaded my case to the customs officer. Tears streaming, I told the officer I truly was Mozambican and needed to get home. Finally, Francisco, our senior Mozambican administrator, managed to reach top government officials, and I was permitted into the country. I heard young men calling out, "Mama Aida, great to see you!" I used to work with them on the streets, and now they worked at the airport. The customs agent remarked that my story must be real; I am a Mozambican mama.

If I hadn't started my journey home when I did, I wouldn't have made it back to Mozambique for many months. I would have been isolated from my husband and unable to lead our physical and spiritual relief efforts for tens of thousands of internally displaced people. The Lord is in control. He had assignments ready for me at each stage. We may not always understand our assignments, but if we yield to the Holy Spirit, God will use everything, including delays.

God, let me be full of Your presence. You've called me to shift the atmosphere because I'm full of the Holy Spirit. Let me carry shalom, supernatural peace, into the chaos of the situations around me.

- Listen and wait for the Holy Spirit to show you what to do: "The mature children of God are those who are moved by the impulses of the Holy Spirit" (Romans 8:14).

- Don't complain. Ask God to show you your assignment: "Guide me into the paths that please you, for I take delight in all that you say" (Psalm 119:35).

- Obey and move: "Loving me empowers you to obey my commands" (John 14:15).

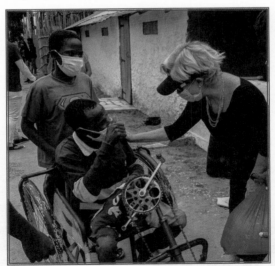

Heidi greeting a friend while distributing spiritual and physical food during the COVID-19 pandemic

Quitting Is Not an Option

Though we experience every kind of pressure,
we're not crushed. At times we don't know what to do,
but quitting is not an option.

2 CORINTHIANS 4:8

Our dream going into 2020 was to open Iris University after fifteen years of spiritual and academic preparation, construction, and extraordinary team effort. Instead, our second university defense was suddenly canceled as a result of internal political conflicts. As we mentioned, the war in our province greatly accelerated. And because of COVID-19, national borders closed, our schools closed, and our bases were strictly quarantined.

The Lord continued to bring us hope and encouragement in the midst of the storm. Just before the shutdown, He miraculously sent Nadia, a laid down lover of Jesus, who has a PhD from MIT in mathematics. She gave up her job as a senior software engineer and product manager at Google to serve as a catalyst for the development of Iris University. Because of the delays, Nadia and our team on the ground, in collaboration with experts from the tech industry and academia, had time to exponentially improve the university and help build a robust foundation.

Beyond our academic preparations, our greatest strength lay in our team praying and worshiping in our prayer house, seeking the heart and face of God: "You will seek me and find me when you seek me with all your heart" (Jeremiah 29:13 NIV). Naturally, our prayer house was one of the first rooms we built on campus. As we sought the Lord together, He revealed His strategies for the university. What seemed like endless delays were actually the hands of the Lord. As a team in prayer, we've been given direction on the academic majors that are most needed. Day by day, God continued to reveal His plans and purposes to us. Then, toward the end of August 2020, we received sudden notice that our defense for the establishment of our university would be held in Maputo on September 17, 2020. Iris University passed our defense, and by early 2021, we were given permission to found a fully accredited university. If you don't quit, you win!

Over a decade and a half ago, I was snorkeling in the Indian Ocean when I felt inspired by the Lord to open a university. The amount of work and effort that has since gone into the process is both unimaginable and astounding. When the Lord speaks to our hearts about His future purposes for our lives and our ministries, we do not need to fear the steps it will require to get there. Perseverance is key as God calls us to "run life's marathon race with passion and determination, for the path has been already marked out before us. We look away from the natural realm and we fasten our gaze onto Jesus who birthed faith within us and who leads us forward into faith's perfection" (Hebrews 12:1-2). Nurture the promises that God has placed within you. Cling to Jesus with all your heart and never ever give up.

Thank You for birthing the miraculous in and through my life, Lord. Give me the tenacity and courage to never ever give up. Place Your heart inside of me and show me what I need to see. You are the author and the finisher. Your promises are yes and amen.

- Trust God for the naturally impossible: "With people it is impossible, but not with God—God makes all things possible!" (Mark 10:27).

- Believe God's promises, "For all of God's promises find their 'yes' of fulfillment in him. And as his 'yes' and our 'amen' ascend to God, we bring him glory!" (2 Corinthians 1:20).

- Endure: "You need the strength of endurance to reveal the poetry of God's will and then you receive the promise in full" (Hebrews 10:36).

Heidi and the Iris University team

ACKNOWLEDGMENTS

I first want to thank Laura Taranto, who worked countless hours with love, prayer, and joyful dedication. In the end, we pushed through war zone crises, a global pandemic, countless power outages, crashed internet connections, and my extremely full schedule to bring this book to fruition. Without her extraordinary skill and dedication, this book would have never been possible.

I also want to thank Rebekah Martin, who has faithfully walked with me these last several years as my personal assistant and anointed intercessor. I am eternally grateful for her friendship and her devoted assistance on every phase of this project.

I want to thank my son, Elisha James Baker, for such a skillful job in editing this book.

Thank you to my husband, Rolland, James and Jessica Brewer, and Pascoal Mafuieque for their powerful, moving photos.

Since I wrote this book from northern Mozambique, many of the interviews were conducted online, so I want to thank the techies at Zoom for making this possible.

I want to thank my courageous friends for sharing their stories in such a real and vulnerable way. Their lives are a testimony of God's great faithfulness.

Thank You, God. You've got this.

ABOUT THE AUTHOR

Heidi's greatest passion is to live in the manifest presence of God and to carry His glory, presence, and love to His body and a lost and dying world. She longs to see others laying their lives down for the sake of the gospel and coming home to the Father's love.

Rolland and Heidi Baker founded Iris Ministries, now Iris Global, in 1980. In 1995, they were called to the poorest country in the world at the time, Mozambique, and faced an extreme test of the gospel. They began by pouring out their lives among abandoned street children, and as the Holy Spirit moved miraculously in many ways, a revival movement spread to adults, pastors, churches, and then throughout the villages all across Mozambique's ten provinces.

Heidi is now "Mama Aida" to thousands of people and oversees a broad, holistic ministry that includes a university, Bible schools, medical clinics, church-based orphan care, well drilling, food aid, primary and secondary schools, farms, widow's programs, and outreaches that include a network of thousands of churches and prayer houses.

She earned her BA and MA degrees from SCC, Vanguard University and her PhD from Kings College, University of London. Heidi is calling for a passionate tribe of true believers in Jesus who will pour out their lives for love's sake, empowered by the Holy Spirit to bring people of all ages home to the Father's embrace!